CIVIL WAR
Duet

DAVID BROWN MORRIS

© 2019 David B. Morris

All rights reserved. No part of this book may be used or reproduced in any manner without written permission, except in the case of short quotations used for critical articles or review. Although the author and publisher have made every effort to ensure the accuracy and completeness of the information contained in this book, we assume no responsibility for errors, inaccuracies, omissions, or inconsistencies herein. Any brands, products, companies, and trademarks that appear in this book are stated for illustrative purposes only. Their mention in no way expresses explicit or implied endorsement or approval of the content in this book.

ISBN: 978-0-578-54599-8 (hardcover)
ISBN: 978-0-578-54640-7 (paperback)

PRINTED IN THE USA

10 9 8 7 6 5 4 3 2 1

For Jules

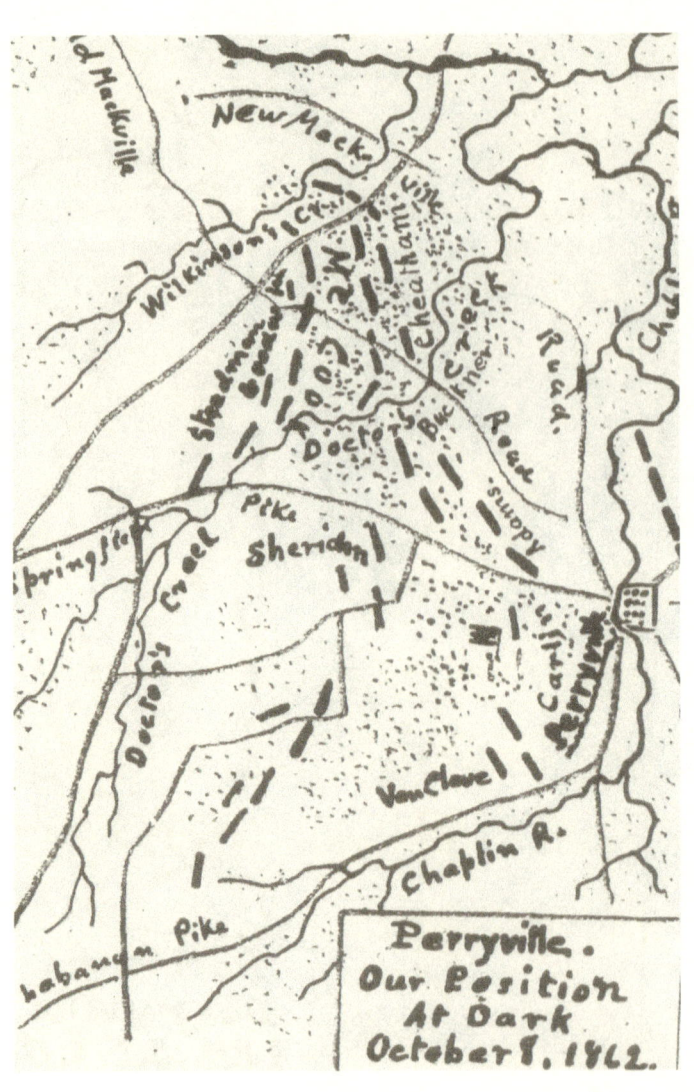

CONTENTS

Part One: The Good Soldier ~ 1

Interlude: Postcolonial America ~ 115

Part Two: On the Road ~ 131

Acknowledgements ~ 229
List of Illustrations ~ 231
About the Author ~ 235

Justus Newton Brown
Age 23

David Brown Morris
Age 75

PART ONE
The Good Soldier

"Can one find the truth in the fragmented and incomplete?
Can one think about history as a collage,
rather than as a narrative?"
—WILLIAM KENTRIDGE (2018)

I have taken my seat to write you a few lines, in circumstances rather peculiar to a Huron County boy. So begins the letter from an eighteen-year-old soldier writing in September 1862 from his temporary camp on an Ohio hillside several miles southwest of Cincinnati. Justus Newton Brown belongs to Company D of the hastily formed 101st Ohio Volunteer Infantry, and he does not know that he will soon be marching south into Kentucky to fight in one of the bloodiest engagements of the Civil War. He also does not know that he will be my great-grandfather. It is high time we have a conversation.

Why now? The time has passed for a leisurely sentimental journey into family history. The country is more divided than I can recall. Racism is on the rise after more than fifty years of steady progress in civil rights. Wildfires, floods, and melting icecaps suggest that climate change—as the result of overpopulation, industrial development, and a drunken spree burning up fossil fuels—now threatens the entire planet. I don't feel old, but the numbers tell a different tale. At seventy-seven, the age when I write this sentence, I have a unique opportunity (in a life devoted to family, scholarship, and looming deadlines) to engage in something like a wide-ranging retrospective dialogue with a great-grandfather I never knew. I have no desire to write a memoir, and I suspect he didn't either, since navel-gazing introspection and a confessional mode don't seem to fit either of us well. My life and the life of the country, however, now appear tangled up together, much as happened to Justus Brown and the 101st Ohio Volunteer Infantry. Perhaps I can bring fragments of our experience into contact—as mutually illuminating shards—not in an actual real-time dialogue but more in the manner of an improvisational cross-century mosaic or collage.

The war in the summer of 1862 is going badly for Union forces. The dark days of '62, some call it. The armies of the Confederacy, in the words of Justus Brown's fellow soldier Lewis Day, have gripped the Northern armies "by the throat." Stunned by the initial surprise assault on Fort Sumter, Lincoln issues two calls for volunteer militias: seventy-five thousand men in April 1861, and forty-two thousand men in May. The regular standing sixteen-thousand-man U.S. army, already depleted by desertions to the South, is no match for the Confederate forces, so in July 1861 Congress authorizes an additional half-million volunteers. Meanwhile, in his book-length history of the 101st Infantry, Lewis Day describes the war anxieties rising almost daily during 1862 and cresting as the Confederate armies in Tennessee and in Kentucky "burst suddenly forth" and "rushed madly northward."

How much does Justus Brown know about the imminent military dangers? He is only a few weeks past mustering in, straight from his first year at Oberlin College, and the Huron County boys count as rank-amateur soldiers. Except for their crisp blue Union jackets, they might strike an observer as more like summer campers. In Ohio, the war remains at a distance, its threats and anxieties still somewhat unreal, or maybe just real enough to excuse the note of bravado or casual reassurance in the dispatch that Justus publishes in the *Norwalk Reflector*, his local newspaper. *While I am writing this I see more than a dozen Huron boys reclining on the ground, in all sorts of postures, to write to the loved ones left behind.*

Who could imagine the carnage ahead? Cincinnati would be the latest strategic prize, and the 101st Ohio Volunteer Infantry is camped nearby to help stop the Confederate advance. Cincinnati matters because it controls the crucial Ohio River supply chain. Its capture, given the complex geopolitics of war, would open a northern front in the Confederate quest to secure the resources of Ohio's southern neighbor, Kentucky, the real treasure. Confederate control of Kentucky—officially, neither a free state nor slave state—promises the additional manpower, supplies, and territory to topple the already tottering Union cause. If Cincinnati falls, Kentucky will surely fall.

"I think to lose Kentucky," the newly elected president writes from Washington in 1861, "is nearly the same as to lose the whole game."

Lincoln has no doubt concerning the importance of Kentucky. He continues: "Kentucky gone, we cannot hold Missouri, nor Maryland. These all against us, and the job on our hands is too large for us. We would as well consent to separation at once, including the surrender of this capitol." Cincinnati, then, controls the fate of the country, and suddenly the colonial dream of a self-governing collection of states seems to depend on Ohio. The 101st Ohio Volunteer Infantry faces a solemn assignment. The outcome of the war will decide whether the United States will even continue to exist as a sovereign nation.

Slavery—at the heart of the war—remains to this day a toxic contradiction at the heart and soul of America. It was a near-fatal flaw in the logic and practice of freedom. The Civil War is far more than an ancient and terminated conflict over states' rights or between agrarian and industrial economies. Ultimately, it plays out a primal antagonism over race that, in its uglier ramifications, continues to divide Americans. Racism in its modern shapes, from unconscious bias to systemic inequalities and routine police violence, might well count as the original sin that corrupts the American dream with lingering nightmares.

Yes, this seems the right time for a personal, cross-century, intergenerational talk with my great-grandfather, who volunteers at eighteen to fight for his country in the dark days of 1862. At seventy-seven, I too feel the country at risk, entering dark days as we lurch toward a self-destructive, anti-immigrant, white-supremacist politics of racist innuendo and race-based hate.

I'm dismayed to realize that I know almost nothing about my great-grandfather. I wonder how many Americans know much more about their immediate ancestors, even in an age of DNA tests and online genealogical services. I could rationalize my own ignorance by reflecting on how little anyone knows about another person. Walt

Whitman, a self-appointed representative of the American spirit, wrote that he contains "multitudes." In an equally famous passage, he describes dressing the wounds of a runaway slave. Poems are sometimes wiser than the poets who create them. According to *Walt Whitman: An Encyclopedia* (1998), Whitman's texts show that "he had little tolerance for abolitionism, that he thought blacks were inferior to whites, and that his opposition to the extension of slavery had little, if anything, to do with sympathy for slaves." I'm curious to know what psychic multitudes and possible contradictions my kinsman Justus Newton Brown contains.

The first thing I learn is that he prefers to be called Newton. His father has a lock on the name Justus, or perhaps some dim Oedipal recoil is at work, which may later surface in Newton's son, Carleton Fairchild Brown. Carleton, like his father, reconfigures his given name, discarding *Fairchild* without a trace. Newton signs formal documents as J. Newton Brown—*J* at least a nod to parental naming—but Carleton instructs his alma mater, Harvard, to remove his offending middle name from all official records. Naming clearly matters, as Newton too writes to his college correcting how he is named. Renaming seems to run in the family, like red hair. My sister, Elizabeth, reclaims her given name in midlife after some thirty years as *Betsy*.

Mere crankiness won't explain all this concern with renaming. Carleton has an upbeat disposition, and Newton (writing in 1907) ends his letter to the Secretary at Oberlin with the collegial closing *Cordially yrs*, written (like his name) in a longhand flourish.

Newton, camped on his hillside, doubtless hears the rumors that Confederate troops are massing for an all-out assault on Cincinnati. No one really knows, not even the generals, whose lines of communication prove highly uncertain and who sometimes simply fail to receive or follow orders. Confederate general Leonidas Polk—a Tennessee planter and bishop of the Episcopal Diocese of Louisiana, with zero combat experience—would occasionally openly refuse orders to fight, a trait that sits oddly with his nickname as Sewanee's Fighting Bishop. Newton does not mention military details in his first dispatch to the *Norwalk Reflector*, which concludes as if written by an eighteenth-century tourist in search of the sublime.

Theories of the sublime belong to my subject in the book that I write as a young scholar fresh out of graduate school at the University of Minnesota, so I feel a modest jolt of pleasure when Newton describes the rugged New World landscape outside Cincinnati (in a no-nonsense, home-grown adaptation of British aesthetic theories of sublimity) as *a very wild looking spot*.

Corporal Newton Brown has attained his slightly elevated rank (a notch above private) perhaps because he has just completed his first year at Oberlin College. The college, founded in 1833, is only a few years older than Newton and—no doubt among its attractions—offers free tuition. In return for their free ride, students during the early years help build the facilities, in a material expression of the innovative college motto: "Learning and Labor." The religious mission basic to Oberlin College also helps account for Newton's choice. Although he spends several years (from 1858 to 1860) enrolled in the now-defunct Oberlin Preparatory Academy, his education at home includes a regular newsletter called the *Oberlin Evangelist*, a series of well-reasoned mini-sermons by the then-president of Oberlin College, Charles G. Finney.

I like the situation of the camp very much. Newton continues writing from his hillside campsite as though this chance brush with sublimity has nothing to do with preparations for combat. Bone-chilling fear is what Lewis Day reports when, for the first time in combat, he hears the order to "fix bayonets." Newton, not yet concerned with bayonets, concludes that the wild hillside scene before him tallies well with *the romance of soldier life.*

Romance? The ancient, chivalric, men-in-armor fictions that apparently color his notions of uniformed military service will soon meet real life. A few corpses will suffice. But not yet. Not with the young soldiers of Company D reclining in various stages of composition. Perhaps feeling a touch of nostalgia, Newton, as if still enclosed in a world of words, closes his first dispatch with an almost formal literary envoi. *Be assured that the Huron boys will never forget the homes they have left.*

Leaving home is a time-honored rite of passage. Distinct from exile or mere wanderlust, the ancient ritual of departure—from Odysseus onward—also implies for its completion a complementary return home. Newton and the Huron County boys are not only writing their goodbyes but also, presumably, anticipating the interlocked rite of homecoming. This imagined return reflects a circular pattern sometimes submerged or denied but almost always implicit in the celebrated on-the-road American spirit. Don't all wanderers long for an imagined return home? Staying put is also an American tradition, however, and homelessness has become almost a recognized socio-political malady. I'd guess that ten high school classmates have stayed put in Delaware for every wandering vagabond, like me, who took to the highway.

Newton's fellow soldiers have mostly never traveled beyond their hometowns. His birthplace, the north-central Ohio town of Ripley, is so small that it's hard to find on maps of the period. In his *History of Huron County* (1909), Abraham Baughman writes that early settlers, a mere one generation before Newton's birth, had to "cut their way into the township through the primeval forest." The single dirt road is often overgrown with brush, impassable to large wagons, surrounded by a wilderness of maple, beech, oak, ash, and walnut. Wolves at night and wild boars during daylight hours make travel dangerous. Newton, who in his teens has already journeyed some thirty-five hard miles east to Oberlin College, counts as an adventurous spirit.

Newton inherits controversy as his birthright—born in 1844, the year when James K. Polk defeats Henry Clay for president in a close contest that turns on the issue of slavery—and I come along ninety-eight years later, born into the turmoil of World War II, on the day (August 11, 1942) when the German SS at Chelmno, in Poland, begins the extermination of thirty-five hundred Jews. A football knee injury exempts me on medical grounds from the massively destructive and divisive Vietnam War: a compound of epic mistakes. The Vietnamese people today refer to the long nineteen-year conflict—a figure calculated by the Defense Department—as the American War. They welcome their former foes today because it is a war that the Vietnamese know they won.

Like many of the Huron County boys, Newton comes from a line of tough, independent settlers with strong Christian beliefs and traditions. They are mostly Protestants—Presbyterians, Methodists, and Congregationalists—who build churches and start religious-based schools while they clear the forests, mill the timber, and welcome the steady stream of newcomers. No easy job. William Stotts is clearing the land when a burning stump flips over and kills him, but his younger brother, Isaac, soon arrives as a replacement. When not cutting down old-growth forests and raising barns, settlers are busy selling the land where Algonquin and Iroquois camped each spring passing through to tap the sugar maples. The white, church-going settlers even manage to appropriate native place-names. *Ohio* is an Iroquois word meaning "it is beautiful." What is happening in Ohio is not always beautiful.

Ohio is a free state, where slavery is not only illegal but also, as many believe, a sin. Beginning in 1803, however, the Ohio legislature initiates a series of so-called "Black Laws" intended to slow black migration. Blacks are required to carry documentation of their free status and to identify two citizens willing to guarantee a $500 bond dependent upon good behavior. They are denied the right to vote, to serve in the militia, to send their children to public schools, to serve on a jury, and to testify in court against whites. *Free,* as a political designation, does not mean that migrant blacks in the free state of Ohio possess either equality or freedom. Newton and his fellow soldiers in the 101st Regiment have the considerable advantages of white skin, but it will also require daily drills and blistering extended marches before the ragtag regiment—lawyers, farmers, carpenters, storekeepers, students, hired hands, and drifters—is ready to fight.

Some physical readjustment is necessary simply in order to march. While officers provide their own boots, most government-issued footwear for enlistees comes in a single shape: two identical shoes—no difference between left foot and right foot—with the soles (at least on cheaper models) roughly pegged to the uppers. There isn't time for preparations or better gear. The placid letter-writers on their hillside will soon face a supreme test of their unreadiness.

Our skin color—I do not say *race*—is among the most significant connections that Newton and I share, as we both inherit the privileges that in America accompany whiteness. (The privileges double for white males, but that's a different story.) We also share the blind spots accompanying whiteness, a legacy of the racism that not only fuels the Civil War but also bedevils and divides Americans ever since. A. O. Scott makes the crucial point in his *New York Times* review of Spike Lee's film *BlacKkKlansman* (2018) about a black police detective who—in order to infiltrate a local Ku Klux Klan chapter—passes as white over the phone. "Maybe not everyone who is white is a racist," Scott writes, rounding to a conclusion that I strongly support, "but racism is what makes us white."

How, then, does racism make whites *white*? And blacks *black*? I don't propose to offer a full response—I'm no expert on race relations—only to identify a few major conceptual landmarks that define the still-unmapped space where Newton and I wander almost one hundred years apart.

Racism creates whiteness in the sense that Euro-Americans come to believe themselves superior to blacks by virtue of race. This new white-supremacist racism differs from the nationalism that allows the English to think they are superior to the French or Irish. It makes skin color alone the badge of superiority. All Americans (whatever their skin color) are now trapped within a labyrinth constructed by the concept of race. We cannot extract ourselves by our bootstraps, as if suddenly minus race, in order to occupy an objective, outside, race-free position.

Future generations may perhaps enter a post-racial era marked by an appreciation of human otherness and a respect for differences, but Newton and I have been thrown into historical moments when race—with all its misunderstandings, hostilities, biases and oppressions—cannot be wished away. Some people today, in fact, are working hard to *preserve* race as an asset in the politics of identity. My claim: skin color and facial features belong to human biology, but race (as a cultural and historical concept) does not. Humans invented race, a vampire-like fantasy that feeds on real blood, and humans have both the power and the responsibility to lay it, permanently, to rest.

Let me be clear. Race, racism, and white supremacy are artificial concepts that prove as material and dangerous as the burning crosses that white racists erect to terrify blacks. They do not arrive with Adam and Eve. They do not arrive with the Mayflower. Race, racism, and white supremacy—like witchcraft and the Salem witch trials—are the product of specific historical and social conditions. Our job now is finally to drive a stake through their bloodthirsty hearts.

Christopher Columbus in 1493 lands on an island that the indigenous people call *Boriken*. He renames it San Juan Bautista, claiming it for the Spanish crown, and soon it becomes an important Spanish colony. The colonial importation of slaves leads to a population that mixes Spanish, African, and indigenous Taino and Carib peoples. Dutch, French, and English traders later add new currents to the gene pool, until Spain surrenders the island in 1898 (along with Cuba, Guam, and the Philippines) to the United States. The name *Puerto Rico* (meaning "rich port") does not exist before 1493, and the island's identity today is inseparable from the introduction of slavery. Puerto Rican life—as a metaphor of global diversity—reflects a highly contingent historical commingling of diverse gene pools and human cultures. We are all creole.

When I'm asked on official forms to state my race, I write that I'm Cro-Magnon. My protest no doubt ignores a pod of nameless hominids who haven't yet learned to stand upright.

AUGUST 1862: CAMP MONROEVILLE

I don't have a photograph of Newton in uniform, but no doubt he looked something like fellow Huron County enlistee George F. Drake (Figure 1).

Drake joins Newton as a member of Company D and, like Newton, is eighteen when he musters in. His photo almost certainly dates from the time when he and Newton enlist, in late August 1862. Indeed, Drake is probably standing against the boards of the makeshift barracks at Camp Monroeville, located some twenty-five miles north of Ripley, where he and Newton remain until the 101st leaves for Cincinnati a few days later, on September 4, 1862. Instant soldiers sent off to instant combat.

George Drake's uniform, buckle, straps, and rifle surely resemble the gear that accompanies Newton on the hillside outside Cincinnati, with the bayonet reserved for special occasions, such as a formal photograph or hand-to-hand combat. The laconic diary that Drake keeps during his service offers an instructive contrast to the expansive narrative accounts that Newton provides in his dispatches to the *Norwalk Reflector* and in letters home. After the horrific Battle of Murfreesboro in Tennessee, for example, Private Drake is assigned to an ersatz hospital with orders to care for wounded soldiers. "Nursing eight men," he writes. "Four with their leg off below the knee and four their arm." No further comment.

This humdrum carnage, with festering arms, legs, feet, and hands piled up outside homes hastily commandeered to serve as operating theaters and amputee wards, is what awaits Newton. Later discharged for illness, George Drake returns to Ohio, marries, and (turning his mournful countenance to good advantage) launches the long line of Drake funeral directors.

Newton Brown, George Drake, and the entire 101st Infantry, marching with their photo-fresh uniforms, do not escape taunts from battle-hardened veterans who pass them on the road. In fairness to Drake, many people look stiff and awkward in nineteenth-century daguerreotypes, which require subjects to hold a pose for several minutes to "fix" the negative. (Faster, cheaper tintypes invented during the Civil War also require a motionless subject.) Photographs, moreover, offer only an external view. The self-reliance that Ralph Waldo Emerson in 1841 praises in the American character means that some of the new citizen-soldiers do not happily take orders from officers whom they recognize as neighbors. Lewis Day describes recruits laying plots against their drill sergeants. Who knows? As he stands rigid for the camera, George Drake may be secretly plotting murder. Unplotted mayhem will find them all soon enough.

Some recruits feel less vengeful than homesick. Others are frightened. They learn that a long drum roll signals immediate danger, and the first long drum roll in a combat situation creates gut-spilling panic. The modern era of professional armies makes it hard to appreciate the sheer rawness of the 101st Regiment's recruits. Civil War regiments are a hodgepodge force that includes a large contingent of the romantic, the homesick, the frightened, and the bilious.

The Huron County boys come to war with mixed motives, but they also offer the spectacle of white soldiers going into battle to contest the enslavement of blacks. Ohio, the third most populous state in 1860, can claim a long tradition of resistance to slavery. As host to various way stations on the Underground Railroad, it embraces a strong religious-based tradition of reform, and thousands of former slaves pass through Ohio on their escape route north. Many no doubt remain. How many? The census of 1860 reports that Ohio has 36,673 blacks, or 1.5 percent of the total state population, and Newton's home state witnesses a number of important events in African American history. Lucy Sessions in 1850 becomes the first black woman in America awarded an undergraduate degree—from Oberlin College, which is also the first American college to admit blacks. Sojourner Truth in 1851, at the Women's Convention in Akron, delivers her famous speech "Ain't I a Woman?" Ohio, however, has miles to go on the march for full civil rights. Its 36,673 black residents in 1860 do not possess legal status as citizens.

War, while well known for bringing about transformations in medicine, also accelerates change in social institutions and cultural practices. The Union army does not accept black volunteers when Newton Brown and George Drake muster in. One year later, however, in 1863, the first regiment of African American recruits from their home state reports for duty: the 127th Regiment of the Ohio Volunteer Infantry (renamed in 1864 the 58th U.S. Colored Troops). Blacks belong to all-black regiments, and 5,092 African American men from Ohio eventually fight on the Union side.

Lewis Day belongs to Company E, and he publishes his invaluable *Story of the One Hundred and First Ohio Infantry* in 1894, some thirty years after the war ends. It helps fill in details that Newton either omits or could not have known, including battlefield maps that sketch out encampments and troop movements. Writing as an historian and former soldier, Day relies substantially on oral accounts from surviving "comrades." Their partial views and incomplete memories recreate something of the patchwork uncertainties that enfold Newton. Like George Drake, Newton simply follows orders, while rumors and misinformation provide the daily fare of camp life. Still, even given their opportunities for unregulated exploits or sinful temptation, the young soldiers in the 101st Ohio Volunteer Infantry are mostly (in the opinion of Lewis Day) "steady, earnest men, as reliable in camp as out of it...."

Neither Lewis Day nor Newton Brown has the benefit of insights that might recognize, beneath the fiery rhetoric about ending slavery and opposing secession, a mighty subsurface conflict over the material means of production and the flow of capital. The agrarian South (dependent on cotton and on the manual labor of slaves) ultimately cannot prevail in war or in commerce against the industrial North. Northern red-brick factories (dependent, to a large degree, on child labor) already signal the unstoppable emergence of a brave new world run by railroads, telegraphs, and steam-powered machines. It will take a long, uncertain war to declare the victor, and the long-term victory may go ultimately to runaway technologies and to the world-creating, climate-changing, industrialized algorithms that confine or constrain us all.

CIVIL WAR *Duet*

*N*ewton Brown's story, as I collect and assemble its scattered fragments, describes a young man from the provinces—still in his late teens as the war begins—caught up in a larger, ongoing, vexed national history concerning freedom and race. The inescapable gaps in his story prove at least weirdly representative of the clandestine privacies in every life, but, significantly, such inescapable rifts do not obscure the dual coming-of-age narratives in which Newton's military service coincides with the remaking of America. The powerful nineteenth-century nation that emerges after the conflict, although still divided and traumatized, differs fundamentally from the thirteen colonies that in 1776 declare their independence from Great Britain. The Civil War constitutes what the pioneering filmmaker D.W. Griffith calls, in the title of his most famous work, *The Birth of a Nation*. The national rebirth, however, remains highly problematic and unstable—despite Lincoln's optimistic claim about "a new birth of freedom"—and Newton's path ahead will prove far from straightforward.

Griffith's openly racist 1915 film was originally titled *The Clansman*, and it somehow earns its status as a cinematic classic despite depicting white-hooded Ku Klux Klan riders as coming to the rescue of a gracious, southern way of life threatened by newly freed black slaves.

America remains a work in progress, perpetually altering its demographics, regularly (for a time) adding new stars to its flag, and always falling short of its own founding principles. The Civil War not only exposes repairable flaws in the social fabric but also lays bare a massive self-contradiction at the heart of America. It is an impasse so complex that the four brilliant, slaveholding founding fathers from Virginia—Washington, Jefferson, Madison, and Monroe—cannot resolve it, either in their personal lives or in the political construction of a truly just nation.

Thomas Jefferson once writes that slavery is like holding a wolf by the ear—equally dangerous to hold on or let go. His analogy, while reflecting his own inner disquiet, considers slavery solely from the slaveholder's point of view. Worse, it equates slaves with animals. As a resident of Virginia, I admire Jefferson's many achievements, not least his bold effort to rewrite the New Testament. (An Enlightenment rationalist, he leaves out all the miracles.) My preference is to set aside the quest to identify heroes and villains in favor of taking a sideways step. I want to explore the experiences of an unknown young soldier from Ripley, Ohio. His encounters offer an indirect entry into the racism that still braids our individual lives with the life of the nation, connecting us across the years.

Racism affects all Americans, as if coiled in our DNA. It shapes and defines us, even if we disavow it. The "n-word," in its unabbreviated form, is branded in our brains. Banning the word from network television does not remove it from consciousness, and some black artists insist now on reviving and recoding it. Even disavowed, racism has infiltrated our cultural institutions. Civil War monuments—often funded in large part by the United Daughters of the Confederacy with an open or covert white-supremacist agenda—now inspire fierce national debate. Diehard racists may eventually rot away in the dustbin of time, but meanwhile we must stand guard. The Civil War does not end with Lee's surrender. Newton carries both a Bible and rifle. He and I are both natural-born optimists, but (importantly) *cautious* optimists.

Flashback! July 1861. At the Battle of First Manassas, Union soldiers drop their rifles, abandon the heavy artillery, and flee twenty-five miles back to Washington, sending the nation's capital into panic. At Second Manassas, fought one year later on the exact day when Newton enlists, Confederate General James Longstreet's twenty-five thousand men counterattack in the largest mass assault of the war, crushing the Union left flank and driving the entire army to retreat. Steady and earnest soldiers would be helpful, but what the commander in chief and his Union generals sorely need is a winning military strategy. Lincoln fires Major General George McClellan in November 1862 because McClellan fails to fight. Major General Ambrose Burnside then assumes command of the Army of the Potomac. It is a long, hard struggle until Lincoln in 1864 gives West Point grad Ulysses S. Grant—a civilian failure who once sold firewood on the streets of St. Louis—full command of the Union armies.

News of the Union defeat at Second Manassas perhaps hasn't yet filtered back to Camp Monroeville, where men from across Ohio gather to muster in. Fortunately, military record-keeping is surprisingly accurate, since there are consequences to account for, such as deaths, pay, desertions, and, yes, pensions. If you credit Google, one woman was still receiving a Civil War pension as late as 2016. Military accounts reveal, for example, that in June 1881 mortician George Drake applies for and soon receives a pension of four dollars per month, based upon the chronic illness he contracts during the war. The records also indicate that on August 30, 1862 Newton Brown signs his name (still visible in the ledger books) for a full three-year enlistment, along with George Drake and the other Huron County boys assigned to Company D.

Company D consists of a captain, two lieutenants, and ninety-five enlisted men. Each company has been recruited from a comparatively small territory. "Most of the boys," as Lewis Day explains, "had friends and acquaintances in the ranks." Like all nine companies (A through K) that make up the 101st Infantry, Company D begins the war with roughly one hundred men. Do all one thousand soldiers assemble to hear their commanding officer? Young and clean-shaven, a country lawyer with intense, coal-black eyes, Colonel Leander Stem does not resemble a typical Civil War general—middle-aged, portly, and bearded—nor does he traffic in military platitudes. He begins his blunt address to his troops by softening its blow before hammering his message home. "Our Regiment is composed of good men and true—men who know for what they are fighting, and when the time comes, the One Hundred and First will give a good account of itself, but in doing this, many must fall...." Then, lest there be any mistake, he adds: "We shall not all return."

Newton, writing in the *Norwalk Reflector*, does not mention Colonel Stem's speech. It is not for home consumption. Maybe every soldier penning letters home from the hillside outside Cincinnati assumes that he will be among the fortunate returnees. Not every tender rite of leave-taking, however, will conclude with a home-coming embrace. In Tennessee, two years after his address to his troops, Colonel Stem is shot and killed at the Battle of Stones River.

"The problem of the Twentieth Century," writes the distinguished African American historian and sociologist W. E. B. Du Bois in *The Souls of Black Folk* (1903), "is the problem of the color-line." African Americans made significant gains in civil rights following the historic *Kerner Report* (1968) commissioned by President Lyndon Johnson in response to ongoing race riots in Detroit, but today these gains have stalled, eroded, and even slammed into reverse. *Healing Our Divided Society* (2018)—a follow-up published fifty years after the *Kerner Report*—highlights three especially troubling facts that illustrate the unstable, backsliding state of racial justice in America.

Fact one: the percentage of African American children living in poverty has increased from 15.6 percent in 1968 to 21 percent in

2017. Fact two: in 1968, some 44 percent of black students attended majority white schools, but over the last fifty years the percentage has declined by half, to only 20 percent. Fact three: the mass incarceration of black males (often for drug-related offenses) has swollen the prison population in the United States sevenfold, from some 200,000 in 1968 to about 1.4 million in 2017. African American men are almost six times more likely than white men to be imprisoned. These facts point to an underlying structural racism and racial bias often ignored if we focus on a few talented black athletes, actors, and entertainers. The dark history of race in America is not buried in the distant Civil War past but continues to haunt and divide the nation.

The color-line, once so clear to Du Bois, no longer resembles a sharp black-and-white border. Racial conflict often devolves into antagonism and simmering resentments, as if a faceless, invisible race-machine mysteriously divides the population into multiple opposing groups, blurred but adamant, with skin color the ultimate marker of deprivation. I belong to the confused subgroup born in the shadow of World War II. We have muddled through at least four major cultural revolutions: civil rights in the '60s, sexual freedom in the '70s, women's liberation in the '80s, and the environmental movement in the '90s. My arrow-like chronology is arbitrary, as each successive wave of radical change tends to overlap with its predecessors and successors. Meanwhile, a quieter fifth revolution—less visible because it is now almost indistinguishable from contemporary life—is transforming social behavior and redefining (especially through biomedical technologies) what it means to be human: the digital revolution. Computers—not equally accessible to everyone regardless of skin color—continue to transform our lives. This new source of unequal access to skills and knowledge defines another blurred but regularly color-based line of division.

Computers are no more than a visionary rumor when I start my final year at Hamilton College in 1963, dreading nothing worse than a beginning course in German. Spanish, my advisor says, has no literature to speak of beyond Cervantes, and I don't know enough to dispute him. As I've already read *Don Quixote* in a Penguin translation, I obligingly take the train to Philadelphia five days each week for a summer course in German. With the long summer over, I am almost relieved to return to Hamilton and two massive senior-year projects: reading the collected works of Charles Dickens and Samuel Richardson. Dickens wrote fifteen novels, and Richardson's mere three novels are multi-tome doorstoppers. Injured as a reader of novels, I turn to poems and ultimately write a book on the early master of compression, Alexander Pope.

Hamilton College, like almost the entire American system of higher education, panics in response to Russia's 1957 launch of the first artificial satellite, Sputnik, and the specific form its panic takes is the institution of senior-year comprehensive oral exams. A feverish obsession to catch up with the Russians in every possible realm of knowledge, but especially in space travel, grips the nation. As a fourth-year student, however, my head is almost entirely consumed by a breakup with my girlfriend (who wants to get married), two immense reading projects, and marathon review sessions for the new comprehensive exams. I do not know what is happening in Alabama, in Mississippi, and in Georgia, where students my own age are risking their lives to protest racial discrimination and racist violence directed by whites against African Americans.

The year 1963 marks a turning point in the civil rights movement in America. Martin Luther King Jr. in front of the Lincoln Memorial delivers his epoch-defining, visionary speech "I Have a Dream." About the same time, the Morris family VW van rolls onto the idyllic Hamilton campus in remote upstate New York, where I plunge out of sight, submerged in the fictive worlds of *Little Dorrit* and *Sir Charles Grandison*. On a cold Friday, as I surface to take my familiar late-morning stroll to class, I am startled when the chapel bell begins to toll nonstop. Is there some malfunction? No. At 12:30 p.m. Eastern Standard Time on November 22, 1963, President John F. Kennedy has been shot.

Thirty minutes later, Walter Cronkite, the consummate television news anchor, removes his signature black-framed glasses, pauses, and in solemn tones, as if reluctant but duty-bound to say what he knows he cannot avoid saying, utters the leaden words "President Kennedy is dead."

The assassination of President Kennedy hits like a psychic earthquake. No one who survives a quake ever forgets the experience. The ground shakes, buildings topple, the heart freezes. An earthquake alters how people act, think, and feel as the material world loses its solidity, and the murder of John F. Kennedy—not a direct cause but the abrupt, seismic prequel—initiates decades of tumultuous social and personal change. My immediate response is blindly visceral. Get out! Get away! Anywhere! Just get out! But where? The extended damage, beyond the immediate circle of the president's bullet-sprayed motorcade, is internal, lasting, and nationwide.

The subsequent live, on-camera shooting of the president's alleged assassin belongs to the visual archives of what has suddenly become a television nation. (Television, I suspect, is the mother of all succeeding revolutions: even computers are inconceivable without the images communicated through video screens.) I consult with my suitemate, Jim Memmott, both of us feeling perhaps what Newton felt in his moment of national crisis. A friend of Jim's, Ron Miller, has just arrived for a visit, and we quickly improvise a plan to commandeer Ron's car for a three-person drive to Washington. Is a road trip the appropriate response to an unthinkable tragedy? Well, not exactly unthinkable. Lincoln, Garfield, and McKinley establish a pedigree for American presidential assassinations. Our response seems, in retrospect, less inappropriate—who knows what etiquette applies to an assassination—than spontaneous and instinctive. We are all flailing in the dark.

THE GOOD SOLDIER

Ron drives as Jim and I plot our route on a folding gas-station map. We are vaguely aware of plans for an elaborate military-style funeral cortege, led by a riderless black stallion, after which President Kennedy's body will lie in state in the Capitol Rotunda. Ordinary citizens will be allowed to file past the coffin and pay their respects. I have no interest in a state funeral. All I know is that I need to be in Washington. It is less a knowledge than the obedience to an unthinking impulse.

President Kennedy's funeral procession makes compelling television. So, too, does the photogenic salute by Kennedy's young son, known then as John-John, an image broadcast and replicated ad infinitum. Jacqueline Kennedy appears in widow's black. Everything is gloom. We drive toward DC in a cold rain and darkness, passing four pals from Hamilton also headed to Washington. Jim later writes an account for the student newspaper, and I rely on it to supplement what I remember from a time I'd rather forget. The city streets are mostly deserted when we arrive early Sunday morning. We park near the Capitol Building and join the line forming—already over a block long—to pass through the Rotunda and view the president's casket lying, as the media endlessly repeats, "in state." Many Americans are making similar plans, as we learn firsthand. Jim includes a detail in his account that seems quietly prophetic of the coming age. A newsreel photographer poses a large black man on the back of a truck, with the Capitol dome visible behind. "The newsman," Jim reports, "told him to lean on his shovel and shake his head sadly."

The day turns bitter cold. We of course neglect to wear thick socks or winter coats. Our line swells into a jostling crowd and previously friendly spectators get surly. Nothingness—as I would describe our non-zen state of suspended animation—goes on and on. Finally, as the once-orderly line of early arrivals turns into a surging human crush completely blocking our view of the Capitol steps, we give up.

CIVIL WAR *Duet*

The turning point comes when a guy behind us starts opening pop bottles (or possibly longneck beer bottles) with his teeth. Impressive. No doubt a great party trick, but I am not in a party mood. Thoughts of a slim, long-haired, honey-blonde coed at Swarthmore begin to distract me. Her photo, sent by a friend and stashed in my desk, blends easily with the image of the wispy French pop singer Françoise Hardy. The folksong 1960s torment impressionable young men, and I am the perfect victim, easily distracted by long-haired honey-blondes. As the temperature drops and my desire to stand in line drops in direct proportion, the thought of a detour through Swarthmore on my return to campus increases. President Kennedy is dead, and I am thinking of wispy coeds? Newton must be grimacing.

Finally, a combination of the cold, the crowd, and the interminable waiting-in-line gets the best of us. Jim, Ron, and I give up and drive to Delaware for an overnight stop at the Morris home.

Fortunately for my Swarthmore fantasy, Jim contrives a separate return to campus with Ron, but my solo-gig luck runs out fast. The detour through Pennsylvania—in the family VW microbus on loan for my return—concludes with a fizzled adventure in blind dating. In karmic payback for disrespecting the decorum of national grief, on the long Monday-night drive back to upstate New York, the heater on the no-frills VW van slowly gives out. I am driving hunched over the wheel to soak up any possible warmth leaking out of the rudimentary heat vents, but a tell-tale numbness begins to spread through my toes, feet, legs. The outdoor temperature drops well below freezing as snow flurries swirl across the blackened path of my headlights. I'm sorely tempted to pull over for a nap. Two classmates died in a snowblind car crash just a year earlier. Then suddenly the flimsy wipers—overmatched by the weather—stop their ineffectual bumpy flapping and freeze solid to the windshield.

Still driving, I lean out the window to hand-clear the accumulating ice. Falling asleep by the side of the road gains ever-increasing erotic attraction. Just when sleep seems irresistible, I feel a trickle of warm air below the dashboard. Instinctively I hunker down, driving half-blind as the snow intensifies. Somehow—maybe the gods favor young idiots—I find my way back to campus just in time to make my 9:00 a.m. class.

Whew! Sleep-deprived and numb, I stumble up three flights of stairs to my room and hastily grab my worn, dark-blue hardback copy of *Shakespeare's Complete Poems and Plays*, making an unsteady dash toward the classroom. Once safely tucked away in the back row, I prop the book in front of me like a shield and hope that I'm now invisible. For a few minutes I escape notice—not called on—but soon I make an alarming discovery. I turn the pages mechanically, in what I trust is a deceptive pantomime, as we begin to discuss an especially rich passage in *King Lear*. Reason-not-the-need. Is "reason" a noun or a verb? I can't tell, but it doesn't matter. Suddenly, appalled, I focus on the page and discover that (instead of the trusty *Riverside Shakespeare*) I've grabbed my nearly identical worn, blue-cover copy of Webster's *Dictionary*.

SEPTEMBER 1862

Early in the morning of September 4—just days after mustering in at the place they call Camp Monroeville—the 101st Infantry boards a train and heads south for imperiled Cincinnati. Colonel Stem tells his troops that their mission is to repel the rebel advance. How does Newton feel about moving from camp to battlefield? He doesn't say. But for a number of new soldiers, the prospect of a free train ride to Cincinnati feels like something of a lark.

The train leaves from the little depot in Monroeville pulled by a steam engine complete with moustache-like cowcatcher (Figure 2). It reminds me of illustrations from a childhood favorite that holds significant influence in shaping my character: Watty Piper's 1930 tale of optimism, limitations, and grit, *The Little Engine That Could*. "We talked and joked and told stories," says Lewis Day about their departure, as if they were on a mission to deliver Christmas toys for all the good children on the other side of the mountain, "and sang songs, and had a high time generally."

The party mood apparently still lingers when Newton writes his first dispatch to the *Norwalk Reflector* from the picturesque hilltop outside Cincinnati that he shares with the other letter-writing Huron County boys.

The reality of war soon sets in, with all its confusions. The anticipated Confederate assault on Cincinnati mysteriously fails to materialize. Perhaps relieved, given their state of unreadiness, the 101st Regiment crosses the Ohio River to a new temporary camp in Kentucky. The move provides a welcome interval for the recruits to acquire basic military skills, but the late-summer heat is brutal. Heavy muskets and hot uniforms turn long marches into survival tests. Soldiers drop by the wayside, straggling back to camp long after dark. Some don't return at all. Confederate guerillas lurk nearby, or so the rumors say, and Company D sends out scouts to find them, with no result. Everyone is on edge. The agenda remains drill, drill, and drill some more.

"We were marched over logs, through ravines, around stumps, through the woods, over fences, into the mud," as Lewis Day recalls, "until we heartily wished every Johnny in the land would go home and mind his own business—we had enough of such warfare."

Bleak moods occasionally give way to lighter moments. On September 25, Newton finds time, during a march along the Ohio River, to write a letter home that avoids any mention of hardship. Once again he sounds like a wide-eyed traveler describing the wonders of a foreign land. *Dear Home*, he begins his personal travelogue, as if expecting that his letter will be read aloud around the family circle.

Nearby dangers weigh less on his mind than the vast distance he has traveled, measured less in miles than in an unprecedented remoteness from family. The new reality of war is sinking in. *I am now far, far away from you, farther than ever before.*

The writerly occasion is too rich to waste on nostalgia or even on ordinary prose. Samuel Richardson, inventor of the English epistolary novel, proved adept at what his eighteenth-century heroines (pen-in-hand at times of high drama) call "writing to the moment." Newton shows that an American soldier can also write to the moment. *But—look! I see some smoke rising up the river. It must be a steamer: I'll wait and see.* He builds up suspense as he holds his audience at home in rapt anticipation (Figure 3). *Yes, I see her.*

There she comes. How fine she looks! I hear music. Louder. Now I can hear the finer parts. There—it plays another tune. Now it has another. It must be the music goes by steam—it has so much regularity. The steamer has a great many men on board, I guess they are soldiers. Yes, for I can see their bayonets glisten. They swing their hats.

Over the top? Why not. Steamships, unlike trains, are still a relatively unfamiliar sight: another modern marvel. The Baltimore and Ohio Railroad begins operations thirty years earlier, back in 1827, with networks of track soon linking most major cities in the north and midwest, giving the Union an important military advantage. Machine-age marvels, however, also include an aura of danger. *Rocket* in 1829 wins a competition for steam-driven engines to power the new Liverpool and Manchester Railway. At its ceremonial 1830 launch, *Rocket* strikes and kills an inattentive official, William Huskisson, an omen of ills to come. As velocities increase, a new medical diagnosis—"railway spine"—soon joins the list of maladies associated with the modern culture of speed and peril. The first spacecraft carrying an American astronaut—*Freedom 7*—returns to earth safely in 1961, but Space Shuttle *Challenger* blows apart seconds after its televised launch in 1986, killing all seven crew members.

Steamships belong in this line of dangerous high-speed wonders. Most have a lifespan of four to five years. In 1844 the *Lucy Walker* sinks on the Ohio River after three boilers explode. Some five hundred steamboats are lost in the four decades following their introduction in America, with a death toll near four thousand. Newton's steamboat sighting is well worth writing home about, especially with hats waving and bayonets flashing. The Union commandeers all the steamboats on the Ohio River, providing another strategic military advantage. The *Allen Collier* becomes a floating hospital staffed with ten doctors and thirty nurses, used for transporting wounded soldiers to military hospitals in Cincinnati. Other steamboats serve as combat vehicles carrying troops along broad river highways with the capacity to launch surprise attacks. They all serve as a metaphor and vehicle of massive political change.

I have had a chance to see something of the world since I enlisted. Newton sounds oddly like a modern military recruiter. His letters home keep pace with his discoveries of a wider world in which he is neither a traveler nor a tourist. Today I shuttle safely between Manhattan and my condo in Richmond, once the capital of the Confederacy, without a second thought, but Newton is growing aware that his journey belongs to the great events of his time, even if as a bit player he cannot grasp their full impact. Virginia secedes from the Union in May 1861, and Mississippi Congressman Jefferson Davis arrives in Richmond to take up residence as president of the Confederate States of America.

A life-size statue of Jefferson Davis now stands atop a massive column on tree-lined Monument Avenue in Richmond, facing other monuments to heroes of the Confederacy. I can view the monuments feeling no immediate threat. Newton as a first-year college student at Oberlin, with Davis alive and dangerous in Richmond, sees his situation in a different light.

The camaraderie of the Huron County boys and the romance of soldier life no longer take prominence in Newton's later dispatches and letters. A serious, even somber, tone replaces the cheerful opening chapters of his ad hoc letters-home bildungsroman. Death, acknowledged as if merely a parenthetical afterthought, is about to make a personal appearance. *If I remain in the army long I shall see and learn something which will be of unreckoned value in future life (if my life shall have a future in this world).*

Two worlds and two temporalities are at stake for Newton Brown: the Here and the Hereafter. I am a stranger to this theology, troubled even by the traditional secular division between time and eternity. I see the planet Earth, imperfect and transient, as constituting whatever we will know of paradise or perdition. We hold the power to damage the planet so severely as to render it unfit for human habitation, which is more than the Bible attributes to the transgression of our heedless prototypes Adam and Eve. There is, for me, no heavenly, eternal Hereafter, only the here and the not-here. What strikes me as remarkable—given Newton's faith in an afterlife—is his attention to things of this world. I'm struck by the conviction that his wartime experience (here and now) will provide him with something—useful later—of great and *unreckoned value.*

What is a value that can be called *unreckoned*? At a literal level, an *unreckoned value* is a value that can't be counted up or fully known in advance. In this sense, it differs from the values that people commonly affirm, such as the value of arithmetic (in counting up cattle) or the value of compassion (in helping others or in building character). Are there values that we know nothing about, values-in-hiding, so to speak, as vital and unknown as the mystic face of God? Newton does not speak about the usual values attributed to war or to combat: a display of patriotism, a red badge of courage, or a testament to manhood. Amid the confusion and chaotic randomness of war, he instead professes faith in what I can only imagine to be an emergent value: unpredictable, unbidden, unforeseen, and unknown, emerging out of apparent randomness like the V-shaped geometry of geese flying south.

Improvisation may come close to describing the trust in *unreckoned emergence* that Newton is taking about—but with a catch. I assume that Newton attributes to God whatever emerges, reckoned or unreckoned, in the here and now. What happens in this life is always, for Newton, in preparation for the afterlife.

Newton and I, despite our differences in theology, are both writers. Writing, I find, requires a trust in emergent values. What emerges on the page may be entirely unscripted and *unreckoned*, like the grace notes of a musician. Words don't always come on demand. "Very few writers really know what they are doing until they've done it," explains Anne Lamott in *Bird by Bird* (1994). Sense—and nonsense—can't always be made up in advance. The finest discoveries may be less a result of careful plans than encountered almost by accident. The *unreckoned value* emerges only in the writing. Newton, living out an unwritten narrative, can only wait for the unreckoned future value to emerge, but at least he knows he is waiting. He knows he must stay alert for something he can't expect, like an entirely unknown species of bird.

THE GOOD SOLDIER

"The president is dead." Walter Cronkite's awful words keep returning me to the roots of downward-spiraling disorder, as if revisiting a traumatic primal scene. We huddle around the TV, watching a newsroom where unknown figures move about in the background—for what purpose isn't clear. It is as if television has betrayed us. The magical new medium (in which John F. Kennedy coolly destroys his clammy opponent, Richard Nixon) has turned hot and evil. It is a memorable day when my parents, adopted New Yorkers, drive from Wilmington to Manhattan for the sole purpose of buying our first television set, at Macy's. I no longer have to pretend I've slipped next door, by accident, just in time to watch westerns on *Frontier Playhouse*. I now have a portal onto the spectacle of dancing teenage girls. A pop music show called *Bandstand* starts broadcasting from Philadelphia in 1952, and for one brief moment of video euphoria, young straight white males get to fulfill their erotic fantasies on screen. Gender fluidity and gay pride are an unreckoned destination, still far off.

"And now a word from our sponsors."

Television also introduces our brains to shifts of consciousness so abrupt and wrenching as to send previous generations (raised on the rhythms of the natural world) in search of medical care. But maybe lifetimes split for every generation and every person. An experience of splitting may be what Newton feels. Any major event—a serious illness, a death in the family, a devastating war—can divide time into Before and After. Nothing from now on, I discover, goes forward without danger of tumbling into this rift opened up by the assassination of JFK.

Time has a way of lurching forward. A few short hours later, Lyndon Johnson is taking the oath of office aboard Air Force One. With secret service agents everywhere, Jacqueline Kennedy stands head bowed, lips half open, almost slack-jawed in who knows what mix of emotions. She is still wearing the stylish pink outfit she wore in the motorcade, now spattered with blood and brain matter.

Nothing to do after Jim and I return from Washington but let the fall semester play out, attending classes as if life will go on. It does. The secret war in Vietnam continues, civil rights marches resume, a new president makes the presidential rounds. Can time splinter as well as split? Newton doesn't say, but the Civil War sends his days as a soldier spinning out of control, and disequilibrium seems inescapable. Mass resistance to the soon white-hot war in Vietnam gives rise to spiraling street protests and near riots that ultimately drive President Johnson from office. Four years later, in April 1968, Martin Luther King Jr.—Baptist minister, civil rights activist, proponent of nonviolence, and Nobel Peace Prize recipient—is shot dead. It is a murder that alters history. The Civil War is not yet finished with America.

Life goes on, or does it? In 1968 I am in Minneapolis completing the requirements for a PhD. Then, on June 5, just two months after the murder of Martin Luther King Jr., Senator Robert Kennedy is fatally gunned down. The 1960s are a national education in violence, mourning, and catastrophe.

No way to put time, split or splintered, back together again. I am married when Martin Luther King Jr. and Robert Kennedy are killed, and this latest assassination is (as my wife, Dee, puts it) "too much to bear." While television crews gear up to smother Robert Kennedy's death in commentary, we pile supplies into our secondhand VW Beetle and drive north toward the Canadian border. Our destination is the remote maze of narrow, interconnected lakes that slice through the wilderness known as the Boundary Waters Canoe Area. As we push off into the wilds and stage our temporary escape, we know there is no permanent refuge. I have a dissertation to finish, with only a few months before we push off again in our packed VW for a job waiting at the University of Virginia that requires a finished dissertation. Today, after two resignations and twenty years as a self-employed writer, I know I'd rather be *around* universities than *in* them. I enjoy working with students, but I've learned that I function much better outside bureaucratic structures that reward my apparent need to demonstrate I am a responsible adult.

I haven't time to write anything lengthy now, but will in a few words, speak of what we have experienced since we left Camp Monroeville. Newton's hasty dispatch to the *Norwalk Reflector* begins with the 101st Infantry departing on its lark-like train ride to Cincinnati. Fearing imminent attack, the city greets their green defenders with an organized dinner provided by local women—well received by the soldiers. Once fed, Company D marches to the Ohio River, while residents cheer and wave handkerchiefs. Then, in good order, the soldiers cross a pontoon bridge built of planks lashed to floating barrels. As if in an obscure rite of initiation, they are leaving the North and entering the South, with whatever emotions are stirred up by a passage into dangerous, alien unknowns. Newton, abandoning his travelogue mode, turns reflective. *It was with feelings very different from any I ever before experienced, that I first set foot upon Kentucky soil. Who could tell whether this soil would not soon be my grave?*

I have some skin—actual skin and real bones—in this high-risk, deadly-serious action. That's *my* gene pool marching into Kentucky. One lucky shot from a Confederate bushwhacker or from a long-rifle sharpshooter, one misstep during a piss break in the woods, and I will not be here to tell Newton's story. As if the idea of his grave in alien Kentucky soil has cast a sudden shadow, his dispatch to the *Norwalk Reflector* breaks off with a sense of danger absent from his earlier reassuring letter home. No more breathless accounts of the first glimpse of a steamboat. The cheering has faded. There is no need to build suspense or to ramp up a sense of drama. The dangers are real, uncertain, and all-encompassing. *We are told that a Rebel army is very near—just how near is not known.*

Richmond today is a small city, some five times larger than neighboring Charlottesville (a small university town where I've lived at two different times as a faculty member). Liberal and art-friendly, with affordable housing that attracts footloose millennials who open restaurants, brew artisanal beer, or telecommute to work, Richmond lies about fifty miles inland from the Atlantic coast, with spacious empty lots and defunct tobacco warehouses available for inventive repurposing. It is also the capital of Virginia. Its population in the early twenty-first century is about 225,000, with blacks holding a five-to-four majority over whites. A former Richmond mayor, Douglas Wilder, in 1990 wins election as the first African American governor in U.S. history. The mixed history of Richmond, which includes the period from 1861 to 1865 when the city serves as the capital of the Confederacy, gives it a special fascination as a laboratory of social change. It is also the only American city that boasts a class-five rapids as the James River tumbles past an island that from 1862 until 1865 held six thousand Union prisoners in a facility built for half that number.

Mayor Levar Stoney in June 2017, seeking guidance from the local community, creates the "Monument Avenue Commission" and charges it with making recommendations about what to do with the city's now-troublesome Confederate statues. The mayor proves clairvoyant. Two months later, neo-Nazis and assorted white-supremacist groups converge on Charlottesville and stage a violent rally. Right-wing protestors and white-supremacist thugs gather supposedly to demonstrate against plans to relocate a statue of General Robert E. Lee. The ensuing August melee—on my seventy-fifth birthday—makes it clear that the well-armed protestors have arrived less to defend a statue than to provoke, vandalize, fight, and unleash chaos. They succeed. Over a tense two-day riot, thirty people suffer significant injuries. The local police stand by, unwilling or unable to intervene—no one knows which or why. One white supremacist rams his car into a crowd of counter-protestors, killing Heather D. Heyer. Television crews catch much of the violence on film, and media outlets loop the footage through seemingly endless news cycles.

The Charlottesville riot shows how a motionless, archaic Confederate monument can animate human passions. In fact, as if the statues could also tell stories, Mayor Stoney charges the Monument Avenue Commission with the mission of correcting a "false narrative" that the monuments implicitly support. What false narrative? Mayor Stoney doesn't say, but most likely he refers to a tacit romantic ideology known as The Lost Cause. The Lost Cause narrative interprets the Confederacy as embodying the doomed noble defense of a genteel and honorable southern way of life tragically destroyed by an overpowering northern military force. This racist and whitewashed narrative promotes a nostalgic, self-serving fabrication—let's call it a cultural lie—that completely ignores the brutal slave economy and its organized oppression of blacks.

Historians tell a far different story about the statues. The statues don't just sprout from the earth in spontaneous tribute to fallen Confederate heroes and their doomed defense of southern honor but rather emerge specifically during the post-Reconstruction era. Their purpose is to bear an implicit affirmation of white supremacy. White politicians after the official end of the federal Reconstruction period commission the statues and pay for them with taxpayer funds for the unspoken purpose of celebrating white-supremacist values and their own newly restored political power. The statues stand as a testament to the racial authority of white southern males. White southern women too, while deprived of power beyond the social sphere, collaborate in this monumental racist charade.

The celebrations in old Richmond start early. On October 26, 1875, the city unveils a statue of General Thomas Jonathan "Stonewall" Jackson as thousands of Confederate veterans and many thousand residents parade through the streets leading to Capitol Square, where the governor of Virginia (James Kemper, a Confederate veteran) waits to greet them. Fifteen years later, in 1890, Richmond unveils a far more imposing equestrian statue in a ceremony that draws over one hundred thousand celebrants. (The 1890 Census lists Henrico County, where Richmond is located, as having a population of 103,394.) The statues thus reflect far more than the political ambitions of a few power-hungry or nostalgic white politicians. Their postwar origin and widespread public approval not only commemorate a racist past but also propel it forward into the future, sustaining a toxic narrative of the Lost Cause that remains in circulation today among people far outside Richmond, like a buried environmental carcinogen.

The monuments today, as if suddenly awakened to recover their voices, serve as a rallying point for white-supremacist demonstrators whose racist project is regularly disguised as a concern for historical preservation, free speech, or states' rights. Passions and prejudice fuel open violence. Many prominent reformers believe it is time to reassess all Civil War monuments, but feelings run high on both sides of the debate. What to do? Preserve the monuments? Destroy them? Move them? Ignore them? Or perhaps the debate and its passions will simply

THE GOOD SOLDIER

run out of fuel. "I'm fifty-four years old," says the always-quotable black basketball star Charles Barkley, in reply to a reporter's question. "I've never thought about those statues a day in my life. I think if you asked most black people to be honest, they ain't thought a day in their life about those stupid statues." Maybe he's right. Do the statues, stupid or not, really matter?

Americans love commissions almost as much as they love parades. In 1887 Richmond's Lee Monument Commission chooses the distinguished French sculptor Marius Jean Antonin Mercié to honor General Lee with a bronze statue (Figure 4). His creation, which now dominates a grassy traffic circle, depicts Lee seated upon his horse, Traveller. Outlined against the sky, it remains a majestic sight, if (a big if) you can truly separate art from racism. Art that promotes or supports a racist ideology—no matter how accomplished the artwork— deserves a careful reconsideration. Lee owned slaves, so racism is hardly an irrelevant issue in his defense of the Confederacy. Four of the first five U.S. presidents, however, also owned slaves, while many rank and file Confederate soldiers—who held fast to white-supremacist values—owned neither land nor slaves. Small wonder that the monuments raise questions that go beyond assigning praise or

blame. A lone rider silhouetted against the sky and elevated high on a pedestal no doubt commands significant aesthetic and existential power when considered solely as an image.

But this is no nameless, anonymous rider—man, horse, sky—or a figure for the isolated human condition, or even a reminder of the time when commanders once rode into battle on horseback.

Ignorance (supposing I knew nothing about Lee or the Civil War) is a poor defense of the Richmond monuments. Statues on public ground—paid for and maintained with public funds—are a public trust. We are not required to endorse the errors of our predecessors, but in fact bear the responsibility for making corrections. What civic virtue is served by the continued public display of an image that many people in the black community—and many whites—find racist, offensive, and hurtful? In fact, we know very well what the Confederate statues represented to the racist politicians who once authorized them, and we know what they signify to racists today who celebrate them as a monument to white-supremacist power. For many African Americans, slavery remains an open wound. How can I subtract such knowledge from my understanding?

My lighthearted suggestion for resolving the monument debate—in an unpublished letter to the *Richmond Times-Dispatch*—is to remove the generals but preserve the horses. The horses hurt no one, at least not intentionally, which cannot be said for the generals. Animal rights activists might object to the bridle? OK. Remove the saddles and bridles too. It will doubtless take another two hundred years before humans are willing to give up our anthropocentric biases and devote our public spaces to an entirely apolitical and biocentric celebration of the horse.

The monument debate, if I may slip out of satire, shows how far race and racism still matter in everyday American life. Ironically, Lee himself after the war opposes commemorative statues, on the grounds that they perpetuate the memory of bloody strife. He didn't mention that those memories can also provoke new strife, and Civil War monuments are not unique in stirring up conflict. New York City recently appointed a commission to rethink the commemorative artifacts in Columbus Circle, belatedly recognizing that the Spanish conquistadors committed unspeakable atrocities against the indigenous peoples whose land they stole. Many voices have a stake in the debates over public monuments—from historians and politicians to the descendants of slaves—but the debate in Richmond comes down to questions about race and racism. Race, racism, and slavery are what bring Newton Brown to Kentucky in the hot late summer of 1862.

All we have to do is to keep ready to start the minute the word comes. We keep five days' rations constantly on hand and are under marching orders. This means that we may move, but implies no certainty of it.

It never occurred to me, until I started following Newton's footsteps, that the Civil War reinvents baseball. Baseball! Writing from his new temporary camp in Kentucky, where he waits in readiness and uncertainty, Newton does not mention that the soldiers in Company D play baseball. Lewis Day reports that the men in Company E—to which he belongs—play "muggins," a variant of dominoes, and only "extreme fatigue," he writes, will keep them from playing. Muggins doesn't require a playing field and so holds clear practical advantages, but it is baseball that occupies a special place in Civil War lore (along with campfire music) as a means of whiling away the time free from drills, marches, skirmishes, and mortal combat. It is Union soldiers who are largely responsible for transforming baseball from a northern city street game (played with wide local variations) into an organized national sport with standard regulations.

Transformed during the Civil War, baseball emerges as the consensus "national pastime," not just another game or a means of whiling away the time but a serious competition almost synonymous with the nation. Walt Whitman is a baseball fan, and so is Lincoln.

Baseball, until I graduate from high school as the catcher on our varsity team, is what (jobs aside) consumes my late summer afternoons.

Newton, with life-threatening duties on his mind, gives no evidence of an interest in sport. He carries a Bible on marches, in order to read during moments when the company pauses to rest. Bible reading, as a practice at the heart of Protestant Christianity, differs from congregational worship in affirming a solitary, personal relationship between the individual reader and the word of God. Above all, it is an activity endowed with the Victorian "high seriousness" that Matthew Arnold soon establishes as the hallmark of an elevated mind. Bible reading, as a serious solitary pursuit, is almost the opposite of play and pastimes. Growing up, I play baseball with my neighborhood pals so late into the darkness that batters can barely see the pitcher. The ball looms up suddenly out of the murk. Our games rarely conclude with a winner but simply stop, abruptly, often (after one last mighty crack of the bat) when the tattered cover flies off and the ball unravels in a rolling trail of string.

Delaware, half slave and half free during the Civil War, remains divided and anxious as I am growing up. I attend segregated schools. I see no black students K–12. We learn as elementary students to crouch under our desks in anticipation of a nuclear attack from an enemy vaguely described as Communist. I also have no clue where to locate the next threat to world peace, Vietnam, on the geopolitical globes—suspended in a metal stand—that come as a bonus when you buy a set of encyclopedias: a required purchase in white, middle-class homes where parents prepare their offspring for college-entrance exams, upward mobility, and clean carpets. (Encyclopedia salesmen sometimes double dip by selling vacuum cleaners: another wonder of the postwar consumer culture.) Parental anxieties trickle down. I talk my parents into signing me up for a speed-reading course so that, like my classmates, I too can finish *War and Peace* in three hours. This new neurosis is sadly wasted on me, since I find I prefer to read slowly. I have no interest in cerebral, indoor games like chess. Mostly, I'm outside playing baseball.

I know nothing then not only about Vietnam, which globes issued before 1949 identify as French Indochina. I also know nothing about Newton Brown. I learn about Newton only in 1996, in my mid-fifties, when our family Christmas presents from my brother Mike consist of bound copies of his research into Newton's life, complete with appendices: *J.N.B.* By contrast, I know almost everything about the 1950 Philadelphia Phillies, who improbably make it to the World Series. A night game at Shibe Park—a grim brick monolith built in 1909—counts as male adolescent enchantment. We climb up dark metal staircases amid blackened industrial crisscross beams until, suddenly, we emerge into a dazzling scene of bright lights and green grass. The reddish-brown infield dirt, swept level with a mat of twisted cables, looks like the floor of paradise. The players are demigods in red-and-white pinstripes. Smoky Burgess, Stan Lopata, Richie Ashburn, Willie "Puddin' Head" Jones. I don't see their whiteness—or my own.

There are no blacks on the 1950s Phillies "Whiz Kids" team. It is only in 1947 that Jack Roosevelt "Jackie" Robinson breaks major-league baseball's color-line. Baseball, however, reaches back much further in the annals of segregation. Albert G. Spalding, the nineteenth-century entrepreneur who makes a fortune selling bats and gloves, writes that baseball "had its early evolution when soldiers, North and South, were striving to forget their foes by cultivating, through this grand game, fraternal friendship with comrades in arms." The hype contains its grain of truth, despite its failure to mention race. It is the "New York" version of the game that catches on with Union troops and even finds a place in Confederate prison camps, where Union prisoners sometimes challenge their guards to nine innings of friendly competition.

The game continues to change. In the early years, teams get to decide whether one-bounce grounders will count as outs, while pitching soon evolves from underhand delivery (letting batters put the ball in play) to overhand fastballs and curves in pursuit of strikeouts. "No human mind," says Spalding, perhaps leaving a door open for the mind of space aliens, "may measure the blessings conferred by the game of Base Ball on the soldiers of our Civil War." So claims the first super-salesman of American sport. Unlike Spalding, Newton no doubt restricts the category of "blessings" to whatever gifts or grace come freely from the hand of God. I have no evidence that Newton ever plays baseball—or takes Carleton on an adult father-son outing to see a game at Shibe Park—but I hope he would forgive me for remembering my two putouts and an assist as the Mount Pleasant Senior High baseball team pulls off its only recorded triple play.

Who is Jim Crow? Even Jackie Robinson might have asked that question about the figure whose name is synonymous with the legal oppression of blacks in America following the Civil War. Today "Jim Crow" mostly refers to lingering attitudes and prejudice that originate in the period soon after Reconstruction, when the defeated Confederate states (finally free from required federal oversight) pass laws and regulations enforcing racial segregation. Even public drinking fountains are segregated into whites-only and blacks-only dispensers, while ordinances require blacks to sit in the back of public buses. As the name for this increasingly distant past, Jim Crow has mostly lost its original meaning and survives as a dusty abstract label, like the Defenestration of Prague. *Defenestration* is a euphemism for political assassinations achieved by throwing someone out of a high window, as happens twice in the modern history of Bohemia. Jim Crow—as the designation for a political period and ongoing racial attitudes—masks an equally specific and grotesque origin.

The name Jim Crow derives from the crude, racist, degrading black character who appeared in American minstrel shows, performed in blackface by white actors. In the 1830s, actor Thomas "Daddy" Rice  introduces the new character by name in a song-and-dance number entitled "Jump Jim Crow," and other minstrel performers soon adopt Jim Crow as a stock character. Minstrel shows prove wildly popular, especially in northern states, which alone indicates how far racism in America extends beyond the slaveholding South, and the popularity of live minstrelsy for almost one hundred years gives Jim Crow a long-standing nationwide status. In 2019 news media express shock when a photo from his 1984 medical school yearbook appears to show the current white governor of Virginia, Ralph Northam, in blackface. His later denial can't negate the fact that *someone* in his medical school class is wearing blackface, accompanied by a white-robed classmate topped with the conical, pointed hat of a Ku Klux Klansman. Sadly, I know from published research that racism has a long and repellant history in American medicine. What shocks me is an image of the crude, degraded, and degrading figure that Americans once routinely associated with the name Jim Crow (Figure 5).

The blackface caricature exposes how white audiences view black males, especially during the period from 1850 until 1910 when minstrel shows are a mainstay of popular entertainment.

Blackface minstrelsy, as scholar Eric Lott demonstrates in *Love and Theft* (1993), involves a complicated and ambiguous white appropriation of black culture, where attraction and revulsion play unequal roles, unlike outright mockery or abject degradation. No doubt. I grow up in a 1950s culture where white singers routinely "cover" songs released by black artists, in a form of cultural appropriation (or theft) designed to make such work acceptable to a large, commercial, white audience. Elvis Presley's 1956 hit "Hound Dog" sells ten million records and launches his gospel-based career as a transgressive rock star, but few white teens know that it covers a 1952 blues recording by Willie Mae "Big Mama" Thornton. I see little beyond the coarse expression of white racism in the loose-jointed, shuffling, shucking, tumbledown, rags-and-tatters figure of Jim Crow.

The image of Jim Crow today is a self-evident outrage, unlike Richmond's majestic horseback statue of General Lee. We should probably consider them locked together, however, in the history of racism in America. The dignified elevation conferred upon a Confederate general, that is, accompanies and depends upon the corresponding abjection and degradation conferred upon freed black slaves. Images can convey as much cultural power as laws. I am not in favor of blowing up statues, pulling down monuments, or destroying the historical record. A democracy, in order to represent the people, must understand, accept, and correct its errors. Racism and white-supremacist violence have no rightful place in the dialogue about American values. It is easy, however, to assert that we reject racism. The hard question is *how to do it*.

Slavery once so thoroughly wove racism into everyday American life that the grinning, grotesque image of Jim Crow might just pull us up short with a healthy jolt. Minstrel shows turned racism into mainstream entertainment. Baseball relegated blacks to the Negro Leagues. Jim Crow portrayed African American males as visibly inferior to whites: shiftless, devious vagrants richly deserving whatever punishment or discipline the white world might impose upon an inherently substandard race. Racial discrimination is still alive and well today, despite significant, if interruptive, local and national progress in race relations. The forgotten image of Jim Crow can serve to remind us how far we have come—and how much farther we have to go.

All we have to do is to keep ready to start the minute the word comes. That's all? *All* is a lot harder than it sounds.

The word has not yet come. Meanwhile, as Newton and Company D continue to wait, Frederick Douglass—former slave, author, orator, activist, statesman—is hard at work in a personal rebuke to racism and to the imagery of Jim Crow. His forceful gaze, dignity, inner strength, and eloquence hold white audiences spellbound as he delivers passionate speeches promoting the abolitionist movement. Eloquent personal testimony is not his only means of educating white northern audiences about the evils of slavery. Douglass, according to the National Park Service, is the most photographed American of the nineteenth century, and he employs the new medium of photography to create an alternative to the minstrel-show imagery of blacks. Smiles are hard to maintain during a long photographic session, but Douglass has other reasons for demanding that no image or photo will show him smiling. A stern dignity—befitting a well-dressed, successful man of stature—is what he wants to portray (Figure 6).

His portrait also suggests the uprightness of a man who knows that he has been wronged—and who refuses to bend. The issues of human rights that he stood for (and the crimes that he stood against) are no smiling matter. His photographs, carefully staged, appear only following 1845, when he publishes his autobiography, *Narrative of the Life of Frederick Douglass, An American Slave*. It is the book that propels him into national prominence and, like *Uncle Tom's Cabin* a few years later, helps to alter the representation of blacks and to redirect the national discourse on slavery.

Any brief account of Douglass's exemplary life (1818–95) fails to do justice to his talent, charisma, courage, independence, and religious faith. He expresses his guiding principles in the motto he chooses for the abolitionist newspaper, *North Star,* which he starts in 1847 after he escapes from slavery in Maryland: "Right is of no Sex—Truth is of no Color—God is the Father of us all, and all we are Brethren." He is an early and strong supporter of women's rights. When the anti-slavery zealot John Brown tries to recruit him for an armed, violent slave uprising or rebellion, Douglass considers the offer—but, trusting then in nonviolent change, reluctantly decides not to join. His choice proves fortunate. Brown, seeking rifles for his race war, is executed soon after his failed 1859 raid on a federal arsenal. Douglass later regrets his decision to reject an association with Brown, as he comes to see that violence appears to be the only means left to root out the evil of slavery. He fully supports the Union war effort.

It is only in 2013 that a life-size statue of Douglass is finally dedicated in the United States Capitol. It represents him as an orator, standing, with no pedestal to provide visual grandeur and physical elevation. I wonder how many visitors to the Capitol have found it—or how many visitors to Washington find their way to Cedar Hill, his final residence, now preserved as a National Historic Site. It is Frederick Douglass who gives Americans an early model of a powerful, eloquent, public black man. Anti-Jim Crow. A distinguished African American and former slave, he raises his voice against slavery, racism, and sexism in a way that commands respect. His late-arriving statue in Washington reminds us that monuments express significant public choices about whom to commemorate and about where, when, and how to commemorate them. Monuments implicitly ask who

THE GOOD SOLDIER

authorized a particular act of commemoration—and why.

Douglass, as historian David W. Blight puts it, is a distinctively American "self-made hero." Blight in his esteemed biography *Frederick Douglass: Prophet of Freedom* (2018) notes that Douglass—in an era when many slaves have only a first name applied by the slaveholder—takes his surname from a novel by Sir Walter Scott. Other self-made heroes of the time would certainly include Lincoln, Whitman, and Grant, in a legacy that continues into the present. Newton Brown offers a non-heroic instance of this national passion for self-invention. In the case of Douglass, I happily make an exception to my general dislike of heroic narratives. Yes, the hero is a mythic figure with a thousand faces, but mythic heroes are usually one-sided and simplistic exaggerations in whom human traits become superhuman. I equally resist one-sided and simplistic narratives of *anti*-heroes, who tend to exaggerate our darker human capacities, and I prefer to think about the innumerable forgotten or unheralded figures left standing in the shadows, whose faithful actions and service (never rising to the level of individual heroism or Homeric grandeur) prove indispensable to the vital, larger public movements in the direction of equality and real—meaning imperfect but inclusive—freedom.

Newton even in the privacy of letters home does not engage in personal criticism or derogatory comments. He refers to enemy soldiers as Rebels, but without insult or malice, and he never speaks ill of his fellow soldiers. There is only a single exception to this general rule of upbeat, respectful silence. He hates Copperheads.

Copperhead is the term applied to Northern Democrats who favor compromise and accommodation with the secessionist Confederacy:

peace at any cost, even if the cost of peace is a reptilian accommodation with slavery. Newton and the Huron County boys regard such Copperhead appeasement as back-stabbing treachery. But it gets worse. Some Copperhead politicians in their support for a compromise with the South also openly urge Union soldiers to desert. Copperhead allies in the press, performing another variation on betrayal, regularly depict President Lincoln as a tyrant trampling on the liberties of Americans. At times they add some openly racist venom, depicting Lincoln as a black tyrant. Both sides in the Civil War speak openly of betrayal. Lewis Day writes that every soldier in the 101st Regiment hopes to return home "after aiding to save his country from the avalanche of treason that seemed ready to engulf it." Treason, however, is a political term. Betrayal implies a very personal treachery.

Newton may feel an extra sense of animus because the national Copperhead faction is headed by two Democratic congressmen from Ohio: Alexander Long and the notorious Clement L. Vallandigham.

Ohio politics in the 1860s is downright poisonous in the Copperhead viper pits. "The public has already been informed of the treasonable and insurrectionary assemblage of certain copperheads in Holmes County"—so reads a notice from the Ohio Executive Department in 1863—"and that a military force has been dispatched to enforce the service of the writs issued against the ringleaders, and to disperse the belligerent assemblage which had been armed to resist the laws." Republican prosecutors in 1864 go so far as to accuse prominent Copperheads of treason. Public trials fill the newspapers with a rhetoric of treason and betrayal that is more than words. On April 14, 1865, shortly after delivering a speech in which he favors giving blacks the right to vote, President Abraham Lincoln is fatally shot.

The murder of Lincoln is not a lone act, carried out by a single gunman for personal reasons, but the centerpiece of a coup d'état by pro-slavery Confederate sympathizers. It begins as a kidnap plan, but the plotters soon decide to assassinate Lincoln as well as to murder Vice President Andrew Johnson and Secretary of State William H. Seward. It is nothing less than a grand design to destabilize and overthrow the American government. The grand design fails. Seward is only wounded, and Johnson's assassin loses his nerve. Ultimately the five co-conspirators are caught, tried, and executed.

But I am jumping ahead again. Lincoln begins his presidency in 1861, and in 1862 Newton is still camped in Kentucky, awaiting orders. This much I know, or think I know. I get seriously confused when it comes to time. Maybe time isn't the regular, tick-tock metronome that we imagine but rather sputters and pulses, speeding up or slowing down. Maybe, like the space oddities in quantum physics and in astrophysics, there is quantum time or astro-time, time pockmarked with nonlinear temporal events, where jumping ahead in time proves as meaningless as jumping ahead in space—as if we are astronauts tumbling in zero-gravity time. The image of time as an arrow always pointing forward—from past to future—fails to account for significant exceptions. In *Entanglements* (2017) Crispin Sartwell identifies six philosophies of history, ranging from simple linear, before-and-after patterns and familiar circular patterns to complex and truly odd configurations, which he calls loop theory, time bang, and loop spiral.

Sartwell particularly likes the image of time as a cylinder of connected loops moving in a massive spiral: "not making any particular progress forward or upward, but blossoming or expanding outward, more complex with each spiral because of the accretion of events." I get dizzy from all this quantum-like spinning, but I can't help thinking that Sartwell is onto something. Meanwhile Newton, in addition to Copperheads, has everyday linear and circular time to occupy him, as nightfall gives added cover to bushwhackers and sharpshooters

"Time is but the stream I go a-fishing in," writes Thoreau in a folksy philosophical image. The meaning applies both to the stream and to the leisure activity of fishing, in contrast to time measured in workdays and workweeks. Industrial punch clocks are a nineteenth-century invention—the first patent is granted in 1888—but Thoreau and Whitman both like to depict themselves as unhinged from the labor market, loafing and fishing. The stream provides more than an image of leisure, however. Thoreau imagines that the fast-moving waters of time occasionally permit a glimpse of unmoving eternity, figured in the stable streambed. Newton would side with Thoreau, preferring a Christianized split between earthly time and heavenly timelessness. I prefer non-binaries: time as prone to eddies and vortices, interruptions in the flow, mystical visions, acceleration, long stretches when nothing happens, or, possibly, alien abductions. I don't discount reports of children who remember past lives, and I know what people mean who say that suddenly—as they locked eyes across a crowded room—time stood still. Eternity I don't get. But no matter what image you prefer—stream, arrow, vortex, loop spiral—I readily concede that it is foolhardy to neglect prosaic before-and-after sequences, like the whiz and thud of a bullet hitting home.

The car carrying President Kennedy on November 22, 1963, turns off Main Street at the Dealey Plaza in Dallas as shots are fired from an elevated warehouse, at 12:30 p.m., EST. It is a moment when, from a psychological perspective, it seems appropriate to say that time suddenly stood still.

Duets imply a collaboration between two performers, often following the same score or script, but I like to think that the presence of two performers also doubles the possibilities for improvisation. One performer may follow the script—but a second performer introduces a new element of the unpredictable. Unplanned collaborative rhythms and syncopations may emerge, as in a jazz session, or spontaneous harmonies and dissonance as performers respond to each other in the moment. Music is not the only arena where the responsiveness built into a duet comes into play. Socrates distrusts writing precisely because it won't answer back. His spoken dialogues, although committed to writing by Plato, link him with older oral traditions of philosophy. Writing, as Socrates sees it, utters its statements and then retreats into silence. In oral discourse, by contrast, Protagoras can't get away with his dubious sophistical claims when Socrates questions him directly. Moreover, face-to-face interrogations require human contact and tact, unlike the kite tail of blog posts in which claims and counterclaims pass each other like ships in the night. Writing is my medium, for better or worse, but the written word (in its semipermanence) permits an artificial contact in which Newton and I may, at least in principle, subvert or circumvent a monological, single-voiced, unmediated writerly stance.

Even this metaphorical duet with my kinsman Newton Brown—which more visually inclined readers might describe as a narrative collage—enfolds far more perspectives than I will ever know. Readers necessarily understand writings within the context of their own cultural era and personal experience. Perhaps our kinfolk many generations removed from Newton and from me—or other unknown, unimaginable readers—will add their individual perspectives to the text as, in reading, they transform our two-person dialogue. A writerly duet, in this sense, is also a secret choral work.

A soldier's wounds depend mainly on the weapons employed, from arrows to swords to pistols. The Civil War introduces newly improved methods for inflicting pain. Painful, debilitating wounds are often more effective than death as an instrument of war and terror. Of course, artillery shells remain a battlefield staple during Newton's enlistment, especially as they provide tactical cover for an advancing force. Shells exploding in your immediate vicinity can wipe out a dozen men. The newest battlefield terror, however, is designed to produce at least as many casualties as deaths, and it functions in tandem with innovative Austrian rifled-bore long muskets. Older smooth-bore muskets firing round lead balls are still in service, inaccurate at long distance but useful in close combat. Austrian rifles, which make their first appearance in America during the Civil War, are both more accurate than smooth-bore muskets and capable of firing at a higher velocity. Crucially, they permit soldiers to replace the older round ammunition with new, conical, and (here comes the diabolical link with pain) limb-splintering Minié balls.

The Minié ball, designed in 1847 by French Army captain Claude-Étienne Minié, quickly assumes its Anglicized name "Minnie ball," but *ball* is a misnomer. The shell, heavier than traditional round bullets, consists of a hollow cylindrical base, a grooved shaft, and a cone-shaped tip. The grease-filled grooves circling around the cylindrical shaft allow greater accuracy and impact, especially in combination with grooves machined into the barrels of the new "rifled" Austrian firearms (henceforth called "rifles"). The added spin and firepower give rise to a rumor that the Minié ball can kill a soldier, pass through his knapsack, and kill fifteen men standing in line behind him. The new cone-tipped soft-lead bullets—far more deadly now— shatter bones and create massive flesh wounds, ripping open thighs and intestines. Shattered bone, unlike the clean wounds from smooth-bore muskets, leaves no option for surgeons except amputation, with or without newly available anesthesia.

Amputation not only removes a soldier from the battlefield, as effective as death, but also requires additional ongoing resources in aftercare. George Drake, when detailed to nurse eight amputees, is no longer a threat to Confederate soldiers. A Civil War photo taken outside a typical makeshift hospital in Virginia showing a grisly heap of arms, legs, feet, and hands does not show the absent military manpower diverted into care. Walt Whitman, searching nearby for his wounded brother, George, encounters a similar scene in Falmouth just ten yards from the front door of the Union hospital where severed human limbs are piled high enough to make "a full load for a one-horse cart." Such piles belong to the new calculations of military loss and gain.

The mortality rate for battlefield amputations in the Civil War is about 28 percent, and the rate doubles for amputees who survive the initial operation. Why? Only five hundred Union doctors out of eleven thousand have experience as surgeons, while among Confederate doctors the number experienced in surgery falls to twenty-seven. Inexperienced surgeons sawing through limbs in ramshackle battlefield shelters without sterile instruments or clean bandages might as well wear black hoods and carry sickles. Soldiers who survive shock and loss of blood face immediate risk of fatal infection. The deadliest postsurgical threat is *pyemia*, meaning "pus in the blood," with a mortality rate over 90 percent.

Soldiers who survive amputation face the additional terrors of phantom limb pain—unbearable pain in the now-missing limb—a weird syndrome first identified by S. Weir Mitchell, known as the father of modern neurology, who observed the bizarre neurological phenomenon as he treated veterans at the Philadelphia "Stump Hospital" well after the Civil War officially ended.

Newton, as he waits for orders in Kentucky, sees wounded soldiers from the 4th Cavalry Regiment packed into the jolting, horse-drawn wagons that serve as ambulances: a sight haunting enough that he writes about it in a letter home. At nearly the same time, Walt Whitman finds his brother (who has been wounded at the Battle of

Fredericksburg) and also discovers his wartime role in tending sick and wounded soldiers. He accompanies a group of disabled Union soldiers transferred north to Washington, where he rents quarters and stays throughout the war, offering comfort for the hospitalized soldiers—"boys," as he calls them affectionately—some, like Newton, not yet out of their teens.

"The expression of American personality through this war is not to be looked for in the great campaign, & the battle-fights," Whitman writes. "It is to be looked for ... in the hospitals, among the wounded." As he comforts the wounded, Whitman is nonpartisan. The numerous military hospitals hastily set up in Washington—no more sometimes than a collection of tents—care for both Union and Confederate soldiers, and Whitman tends them all. The war leaves him with no illusions. Judiciary Square Hospital in Washington is notorious for dumping naked corpses on an adjacent vacant lot. His hours spent in Campbell Hospital and in Armory Square Hospital tending to sick and dying soldiers temper Whitman's native optimism and chasten his role as poet-sage of the new democratic spirit, adding a sober, sorrowful note that reflects his firsthand experience of national self-laceration: a nation at war with its own people as American boys are wounding and killing American boys.

Women too play an important role in the national conflict, as nursing, like medicine, makes significant advances during war. Clara Barton, a former teacher and later founder of the American Red Cross, both supports Union troops with medical supplies and cares for wounded soldiers in front-line hospitals. Dorothea Dix and Elizabeth Blackwell train some three thousand women to serve as nurses for the Union Army—a fraction of the twenty thousand women who serve as paid or unpaid nurses, often within combat zones. The United States Sanitary Commission, formed in 1861 to advance the war effort by reforming hospital care, takes its inspiration and model from the work of Florence Nightingale during the Crimean War. Ohio physician Albert N. Read—father of Ira Beman Read—serves as inspector in chief for the Sanitary Commission throughout the war and receives credit for retrofitting railway cars so that wounded soldiers arrive at hospitals with less suffering. Such advances improve your odds of survival, but the best hope lies in avoiding hostile contact with the Minié ball. Piles of shattered limbs attest to its good design.

Fear is a common bond across space and time. Newton, as he crosses into Kentucky, may feel something like the cold shudder I try to ignore as I push off from Santa Cruz aboard the rickety two-hundred-foot converted cod trawler *Sea Shepherd II*. It is 1990, and we are bound on a direct-action mission in the North Pacific. The captain, environmental activist Paul Watson, is among the founders of Greenpeace. He turned out to be too radical for Greenpeace's fundraising purposes, so when Greenpeace expels him in 1977, Watson founds the Sea Shepherd Conservation Society. Its purpose is to oppose the slaughter of marine wildlife—especially whales. Watson's confrontational methods, which include ramming ships at sea, differ from Greenpeace's preference for symbolic protest. He works far better within an organization (staffed by volunteers and funded by private donations) entirely under his control.

I'm surprised when he invites me to join him on the current anti-driftnet mission in the North Pacific. I'm in Oregon when I reach him by phone, on the final stop of a brief book tour, two thousand miles from my home with Ruth in Michigan. "We're leaving tomorrow," Watson tells me with just a trace of a Canadian accent. I instantly accept.

Our rendezvous point, I'm told, is a dock near Santa Cruz on Monterey Bay, where *Sea Shepherd II* is taking on final supplies for the monthlong voyage. I have no idea how we will meet up, but I don't want to miss an opportunity that might not come again. I know that several groups have tried to kill Watson, so far unsuccessfully. A preternatural calmness gives him an almost posthumous air—as if his death has already occurred—which does nothing to calm my fears. Just before the ship leaves Santa Cruz and on the assumption that I may not return, I mail three goodbye letters: to my parents, to Ruth, and to my amazing college-age daughter, Ellen.

Seasickness soon replaces death as my primary concern. There is so much water, nothing but water, days spent grey and gripped with nausea. I do not share Newton's confidence that I might learn something of unreckoned value for my future life. I just want to get home alive and to write another book. I feel the fear on my tongue with a sour, metallic aftertaste.

Driftnet fishing bears no resemblance to sport or to Izaak Walton's philosophical leisure. Commercial ships lay down a continuous nylon net stretching a few feet below the surface for some thirty-five miles. These industrial mesh curtains of death entangle everything in their path, including sea birds that dive for fish trapped in the silvery-blue mesh. Watson packs the bow with concrete, converting the ship into a high-seas battering ram. His modus operandi is to hunt down driftnet ships and to crash into them. Terrorism and piracy are familiar charges that don't faze him. "We're the good pirates," he likes to retort.

My immediate problem is not with piracy. I have reason to believe that Watson places a higher value on whales than on humans. Even his crew members get no special dispensation, since we do not qualify as members of an endangered species. As the lone writer on board, I don't even have the semi-valuable human status of, say, the cook. We hear rumors that Watson plans to sink the *Sea Shepherd II* on this mission, as it has outlived its usefulness, and I note an acute absence of lifeboats. Don't worry about a life preserver, Watson says cheerfully. The North Pacific is so cold that you'll die of hypothermia within a few minutes. Our chief engineer in charge of keeping the motors shipshape recently left his job fixing bicycles. My fears rise in direct relation to a plummeting confidence level.

Newton has a realistic likelihood of getting shot, which at least he signed up for. At a crucial moment, with Watson on the bridge of *Sea Shepherd II* aiming his cod trawler on a collision course with a Japanese driftnet ship, almost predictably the water pump malfunctions. Watson and his ship are suddenly dead in the water. No worries. He radios to the first mate on the accompanying coast guard cutter, where I'm stationed, to go down to Watson's cabin, retrieve the AK-47 assault rifle on his bed, and start firing. This dicey moment belongs to the full story that I recount in *Earth Warrior* (1995) and precedes the return voyage when we are boarded by the U.S. Coast Guard and read our Miranda rights. Yes, I survive. Once safely back on dry land and headed double time to Michigan, I imagine that FBI agents will yank me off the plane at every stop. The fear takes several weeks to subside.

I happily accept whatever ironies or invidious comparisons accrue to parallels between a seventy-seven-year-old writer (secure in a well-lit study) and his great-grandfather at eighteen marching through the heat and rain, sleeping wrapped in a muddy rubber sheet, and knowing at any moment that he may hear the long drum roll signaling imminent combat. I am grateful I don't have to worry about sharpshooters, guerrillas, bushwhackers, and a midnight call to arms.

The largest historical irony for anyone who associates the Republican party today with spineless legislators and with right-wing, crypto-racist populism lies in recalling that Lincoln is the founding father of the party. In 1860, the Republicans publish their platform, which includes ten declarations of principle that directly address slavery. Here is a sample of early Republican political backbone:

> 8. we deny the authority of Congress, of a territorial legislature, or of any individuals, to give legal existence to slavery in any territory of the United States;

> 9. we brand the recent reopening of the African slave trade, under the cover of our national flag, aided by perversions of judicial power, as a crime against humanity and a burning shame to our country and age; and we call upon Congress to take prompt and efficient measures for the total and final suppression of that execrable traffic.

A provision that prohibits extending slavery in territories not yet granted statehood certainly falls short of a full-throated denunciation of slavery in America. Abolition of the slave trade, likewise, does not abolish existing slavery in the South or even greatly inconvenience slaveholders. The Republican platform expresses a dislike of slavery, but Republicans do not dislike slavery enough to propose declaring it illegal.

The Democrats, with marginally less backbone, fail to support even a modest proposal prohibiting the extension of slavery into undeclared states. High-minded descriptions of the slave trade as a "burning shame" mostly put on display the rhetorical skill of politicians capable of speaking simultaneously out of both sides of their mouths.

Lincoln, as the surprise Republican candidate for president, inherits their platform with its high-minded evasions. Evasion may be a useful tactic for Republicans, since disagreements in 1860 about slavery split the Democratic Party into Northern and Southern factions. The years 1860 and 1861, however, put an end to evasion. Eleven southern states secede and establish the Confederate States of America. Their next major political step is to commence open war with the Union and with its newly elected Republican commander in chief, Lincoln.

Lincoln enters the White House when the nation is splitting apart, and his tenure as president during this long American self-laceration marks him as a near-tragic figure. As contemporary photos suggest, his stooped shoulders and mournful countenance express the heavy fate he must accept. He does as much as George Washington to hold the young country together, but his achievement seems inseparable from personal sorrow and loss, while Washington is often represented as heroic, sometimes even clothed in a Roman toga. Lincoln gives the impression that a national fate has immersed him in what Virgil—in his tragic epic about the founding of Rome—calls *lacrimae rerum*, or "the tears of things." It's important not to overemphasize Lincoln's tragic side. He consistently employs humor as wry emotional ballast, and his favorite dessert (served to visiting dignitaries at the White House) is a colonial American invention: lemon meringue pie. He may be responsible for its popularity throughout Europe. Then, too, at 6' 4" with a size 14 shoe, Lincoln suffers continual foot pain—even submitting to an operation for relief—so it requires some caution to read his facial expressions. As a private citizen, he adamantly opposes slavery, but as president he needs to hold the splintering country together while working steadily toward both military success and revolutionary political change.

"My paramount object in this struggle is to save the Union," Lincoln writes in a letter to Horace Greeley in 1862, "and it is not either to save or destroy slavery. If I could save the Union without freeing any slave I would do it; and if I could save it by freeing all the slaves I would do it; and if I could save it by freeing some and leaving others alone I would also do that. What I do about slavery, and the colored race, I do because I believe it helps to save the Union."

The tragic impasse over the issue of slavery that confronts Lincoln as a president leading a nation split into warring armies will ultimately require rivers of blood. It is a cost in lives that, as president, he cannot avoid, like an encounter with the classical deities of fate and necessity. When he deals with slavery on his own terms, free from military or political strategies, Lincoln's temperament inclines him toward Twain-like affirmations couched in irony and humor. "Whenever I hear anyone arguing for slavery," he says in a speech delivered in 1865, "I feel a strong impulse to see it tried on him personally." A few months later he is assassinated.

Newton in his letters home frequently mentions standing *picket duty*. I head directly to the internet. *Picket*, as a military term used during the Civil War, refers to an advance outpost or guard protecting a large armed force. A broad but scattered line of soldiers constitutes a shapeless human fence set far enough ahead of the main encampment to offer early warning. A picket guard regularly includes a lieutenant, two sergeants, four corporals, and forty privates, and it proves hazardous duty. Infantrymen spread out as isolated pickets are easy targets for bushwhackers. Each opposing army assigns pickets to protect its perimeter, so that isolated pickets often can't avoid encounters with enemy pickets, resulting in deadly one-on-one skirmishes. Newton spends many nights alone in the woods on picket duty—half a mile or more from the main camp, too far away to call for help. He may not be missed until the next roll call if a Confederate bushwhacker succeeds.

Newton seems changed even after only a brief time as a soldier, including no doubt anxious nights in unfamiliar woods. On camping trips, I spend nights wide awake listening for bears and goblins. Newton's letters home no longer resemble a leisurely or excited travelogue but seem more like updates written in fatigue or squeezed into Sunday intervals, after the drills and duties and foraging. Other soldiers write letters to girlfriends or fiancées, and Colonel Stem writes regularly to his wife, but there is no indication in Newton's letters that he leaves behind a girlfriend or fiancée. This absence strikes me as slightly odd because two years after the war ends—in an era given to long engagements—he marries Harriet "Hattie" Augusta Sparhawk.

Were they acquainted before the war? A local map from 1874 indicates that lot 60 in the town of Oberlin is owned by "J Brown," no doubt Newton's father, Justus Brown. Lot 59 is owned by (drum roll, please) Lucy C. Sparhawk. It doesn't take a Pindaric leap to conclude that Lucy C. Sparhawk is the mother of Newton's future wife, Hattie. Newton marries the girl next door, but I'm not positive—despite the map—exactly where their doors are.

Records at Oberlin College show that Hattie is born in Norton, Ohio and that, just before entering Oberlin, she resides in Tallmadge, Ohio. The Sparhawk family (transplanted from Vermont) moves several times in Ohio, and the Brown family, too, moves at least once—from Ripley to nearby Greenwich Station. It is Oberlin College, however, that completes the spiritual triangulation connecting Newton and Hattie. Whatever their possible relationship as neighbors or friends or classmates, Hattie and Newton begin their studies together at Oberlin College in 1861—the year before Newton musters in to the 101st Ohio Regiment—and their trajectories remain inseparable thereafter.

Bare dates provide at least an outline for imagining their relationship. Hattie, one year older than Newton, interrupts her undergraduate work in 1862, just when Newton leaves for Camp Monroeville. They are moving in tandem—and their dance may involve romance. They marry in 1867, just before Newton (returned from the war) begins his final undergraduate year at Oberlin. Hattie resumes her undergraduate studies a year later, in 1868, when Newton enrolls in Oberlin Theological Seminary. By mid-July 1869 they are parents. Motherhood brings new responsibilities, and Hattie leaves off her studies for an undergraduate degree. On a later questionnaire, she describes her occupation as "Keeper of the Home" and doubtless understands her role as a traditional nineteenth-century "helpmate." She and Newton live together for fifty-six years until Hattie's death in 1923, but there are big surprises along the way.

Eight months after Hattie's death, Newton, now age eighty, marries her sister "Mattie."

What's going on? I'm not sure. Perhaps Hattie with her dying breath asks Newton to care for her sister. Newton's brother marries a Sparhawk. Maybe Newton in his eighties figures that the Brown brothers have a good thing going with the Sparhawk sisters. Such dual-sibling marriages are not uncommon at a time when eligible partners in small towns often live close together, schoolmates and neighbors. In an era before Social Security, families feel a special need to look after each other. Mattie, Hattie, and Newton all attend Oberlin Preparatory Academy as schoolchildren, although their dates don't exactly overlap. Did Newton at eighty marry his elderly sister-in-law, Mattie, with the hope of mutual companionship and care? Or did he want to ensure that Mattie, on his death, would be entitled to receive his military pension?

I don't know. Some questions about the entangled lives of Hattie, Mattie, and Newton will always remain unanswered, but I know at least something about how their story unfolds. Mattie (born Martha Alcina Sparhawk) serves as legal witness to Newton's 1912 petition for a military pension. The petition is submitted in Pennsylvania, and her role as witness suggests that she is already living with Hattie and Newton. If so, what may have started as a temporary domestic triangle becomes a fortunate long-term arrangement. In June 1925, one year after he marries Mattie, Newton suffers a debilitating stroke. Mattie clearly tends to Newton during his final days—with money likely running out. After his death, Mattie files her own petition to receive Newton's small military pension, on the grounds as stated in the boilerplate language of the petition (and not necessarily an official medical or psychiatric diagnosis) that he is "insane."

A beautiful symmetry enfolds Newton's life with Hattie and Mattie Sparhawk. Their separate journeys out of Ohio begin with an unplanned detour as he stands solitary picket duty in the dark, awaiting orders. Ultimately—after many twists in the road—their intertwined lives return almost full circle. Westwood Cemetery in Oberlin includes three gravestones side by side. The middle grave belongs to Newton. Hattie and Mattie are buried on either side. The three Ohio neighbors, after their long years of wandering, might as well be holding hands.

The three adjoining gravestones create an imperfect and mysterious erotic geometry. A born romantic, I am lucky to have married two amazing women—Dee Kirby and Ruth Cohen—but what I don't know about women would fill an encyclopedia. Freud's famous conundrum "What do women want?" (*Was will das Weib?*) strikes me as what philosophers call a bad question. Are women a homogeneous group who share a single set of desires? Or is Freud simply producing a quotable version of the male belief—dating back at least to Virgil—that women are an enigma? A better question: what does any individual woman want? The Sparhawk sisters, if in agreement, might want to vote. They might want equal rights and equal opportunities. If so, they have a long wait. I simply lack any specific information about the desires of Hattie and Mattie—open, concealed, sublimated, blocked, deformed, or deflected.

Desire quickly opens upon an infinite regress of puzzling, entangling spirals. How many people—of any gender, in any era—ever truly *know* what they want? If Freud is correct, the unconscious mind shapes our desires in ways we aren't fully aware of, much as advertisers employ hidden prompts and sexual codes—imagistic influencers—that encourage us to desire a particular car or beer. Our desires are rarely pure, and it is rare that our desires are purely ours. The boy who wants to be a fireman or a doctor or a superhero may want what the culture wants *for* him. My variation on Freud's question is just as hard to answer. What does *Newton* want?

Newton clearly wants a life with Hattie and a life with Mattie. Erotic attachments, as a basic human drive or desire, can take many forms, from a mother's love for her child to a soldier's patriotic love of country or a priest's love of God. Love, as a romantic bond, must be what keeps Newton and Hattie together for fifty-six years. Desire, even if expressed as love of family, must be in part what moves Newton (when Hattie dies) to marry Mattie. His religious vocation is far more than a means to earn a living, but he never writes about his personal love of God. Does he love the parishioners whose immortal souls are temporarily under his care? What, exactly, *moves* him?

I freely admit that my desires are centered in the woman I love, whose desires, I'm content to say, will always remain in part a profound mystery. I ask Ruth to marry me eleven days after we meet in LA. We later laugh about our high-speed courtship—I am separated from Dee but not yet divorced—but also respect its force. We know that we belong together. (Maybe Newton and Hattie also know.) Friends marvel at our closeness. Our thirty-year marriage ends with Ruth's death, after a ten-year descent into the slow limbo of Alzheimer's disease. Later, at seventy-five, almost the same age when Newton marries Hattie's sister, I fall in love with Margot Wolf—a professional writer and talented amateur painter—also at warp speed.

My *Blitzliebe* tendencies, I recognize, can prove troublesome, but so can endless delay and overanalysis. The process remains both a mystery to me and an exception. It has occurred just three times over three quarters of a century. Some might say I'm just very picky. OK. I prefer to say that I trust my heart, hope for the best, and own the consequences. Although I'm all for knowledge, especially knowledge about love, what we know continues to change, we too continue to change, and rational analysis takes us only as far as facts and logic permit. I've increasingly come to lean on an intuitive, spontaneous, emotion-based knowing, less analytic than synthetic, making connections rather than discriminations. Followed blindly, of course, any form of knowing can lead you astray, including logic and reason. Self-blinding is never a good strategy, and the love I'm describing—despite conventional images of Cupid—isn't blind. It knows something that it can't quite put into words or divide to fit a Venn diagram. Love and desire are the jet fuel for a risky voyage that can lift you to the stars. The risks are real, and the failures—also real—always hurt.

Before dawn, the hospice nurse in Ruth's facility phones me in Richmond saying that the end is near. I pull on my jeans, race downstairs to the garage, and drive high-speed on the familiar, deserted I-64 corridor to Charlottesville. When I reach her bedside, Ruth has just died.

I sit alone beside Ruth's body for almost an hour. I don't feel sucked down into a vortex of disorienting grief. Maybe, at intervals during an arduous decade spent sharing the daily losses that her illness entails, I have already pre-grieved. She is over seventy, and her skin (pale from years spent indoors in a wheelchair) looks smooth and flawless. Will anyone understand? My visits to her in the well-run Alzheimer's facility where she lived as almost a prisoner always left me feeling hopeless and despondent. On this last visit, I feel strangely proud of her for slipping away into the early morning, on her own terms.

Emerson—lanky, stiff, and formal in his ill-fitting dark suit—offers more than general reflections on love. He delivers an unambiguous personal and grammatical imperative: "give all to love." As a young man, after less than eighteen months of marriage, he loses his beloved wife, Ellen Tucker, to tuberculosis. Five years later, in his debut philosophical meditation *Nature* (1836), he concludes the opening chapter with an abstract account of the mind's power to take delight in the natural world. Then, submerging his personal loss in a third-person voice, he describes "a kind of contempt of the landscape" felt by a person "who has just lost by death a dear friend." Emerson is just such a person. "The sky," he adds, "is less grand as it shuts down over less worth in the population."

On the morning Ruth dies I feel a sense, like Emerson, that the world has suffered a significant loss. Loss, cosmic or personal, does not alter Emerson's trust in love. The human imperative remains clear: "Obey thy heart; / Friends, kindred, days, / Estate, good-fame, / Plans, credit and the Muse,— / Nothing refuse." I am an Emersonian right down to the bone, including his belief in the spirit, or whatever term describes the spark of life visible in Ruth's chestnut-brown eyes. Eros, the ancient god celebrated from various perspectives in Plato's *Symposium* and in the bittersweet odes of Sappho, remains my guide. When Ruth dies, for at least half a decade I lose the ability to write—although I doggedly keep on writing, poorly—as well as the confidence to trust my feelings. Writing too, as a creative activity, falls under the sign of Eros. I wonder if Newton and I belong to the same ad hoc, multigenerational, extended family of born romantics.

Thursday, the enemy were to be seen in large numbers some two miles from here. So Newton reports in early September 1862, as Company D first moves into the temporary Kentucky position they call Camp Stem—just south of Cincinnati and a few miles from the Kentucky town of Covington. They remain there for five days, still marching and drilling and securing their perimeter, "becoming accustomed," as Lewis Day remembers, "to our new mode of life." The new mode includes getting used to the crack of gunfire. Enemy forces lurk somewhere within easy reach of their new camp. Pickets on both sides trade shots all day, usually at long range, with only minor, occasional casualties. It takes a downpour to interrupt the shooting.

Company D has yet to face a massed army on the battlefield. The experience of daily hostile gunshots at least makes them slightly better prepared for the firing ahead. The five-day stopover at Camp Stem brings one major advance in combat readiness: new Austrian Lorenz rifles. Lewis Day calls them, approvingly, "genuine guns." Austrian rifles in fact are the latest innovation in military hardware, and the new imports soon flood the arms market. The Union army buys 226,924, while the Confederacy buys some 100,000. These genuine guns, as Lewis Day continues, pack a punch that makes them "second cousins to mountain howitzers." The Lorenz rifle is muzzle-loaded, like the smooth-bore musket it replaces, but the grooved ("rifled") barrel gives it greatly improved accuracy. The Lorenz comes in three models, for short, medium, and long-range combat. The short-range version is most common, but its improved accuracy entails a significant cost. "It took a good deal of muscle," Lewis Day recalls, "to get the thing out straight even long enough to pull the trigger."

Lengthy drills with the new twelve-pound Lorenz leave soldiers with aching shoulders and produce a cascade of what Day calls "bad words." Swearing seems an almost inescapable byproduct of military life. English soldiers swore so freely during the Hundred Years War (1337–1453) that their French enemy nicknamed them *les goddams*. Newton, I suspect, given his religious upbringing, hoists the Austrian Lorenz curse-free.

Curses may be called for. It takes a full nine-step process to prime the muzzle-loading Lorenz, with a prescribed sequence. One, you place the stock against the ground, for stability; two, you remove a paper cartridge from your satchel and, with your teeth, rip open the cartridge pouch; three, you slide the gunpowder from the cartridge pouch down into the barrel; four, you wad the cartridge paper and stuff it atop the gunpowder; five, you place the Minié ball (tip outward) into the barrel; six, using the ramrod attached to your rifle, you pack the one-ounce Minié ball onto the paper-wadded gunpowder; seven, you remove and replace the ramrod; eight, you grab a percussion cap from your belt pouch and fit it onto the nipple of your rifle. Nine—assuming that you haven't already been shot while loading—you cock your rifle, lift, aim, and fire.

Assumptions are risky. Your hand may shake as you pour gunpowder down the barrel. Bullets whiz and slam around you. If you ram the Minié ball down the barrel before wadding up the paper, you need to fish out the bullet. The Lorenz includes a corkscrew device on the ramrod designed specifically to extract bullets. Newton in his letters and dispatches says nothing about the new rifles. He is far more concerned with tents. In particular, he is concerned with not having one. As the autumn nights grow colder, the routine of falling asleep without a tent in a muddy, rain-soaked uniform transforms a simple pup tent into something like a transcendental object of desire.

The American love affair with guns, which often begins in childhood, illustrates the dangers of misdirected Eros. My mother, Newton's granddaughter, lived with a dime-sized depression in her upper thigh from a bullet wound. Her brother, as a child, had shot her. Accidently? As adults, they rarely communicate. I blame him for a childhood bereft of toy pistols, but my mother is right: guns make poor toys. People wielding toys, replicas, and BB guns prompt eighty-six police killings between 2015 and 2016. In 2014, police in Cleveland mistakenly shoot Tamir Rice, a twelve-year-old African American boy playing with a toy pistol. Toy guns look real, and real guns are sold in

THE GOOD SOLDIER

American discount stores like toys. Lee Harvey Oswald twice qualifies at marksman level in the Marines, and gun shops in the 1960s sell the Carcano rapid-fire rifle he uses to kill John F. Kennedy at the bargain (near giveaway) price of $10 to $20.

Newton, like other Civil War soldiers, presumably carries a double-bladed dagger: a weapon, unlike knives, made solely for stabbing, which is why it becomes the preferred instrument for dark-alley murders. Newton, in addition to the latest Lorenz rifle, thus carries one of civilization's oldest weapons for hand-to-hand combat, once favored by medieval knights as useful in penetrating the chinks, literally, in an enemy knight's otherwise impenetrable armor.

Picket duty provides a welcome, if edgy, alternative to drills and waiting. The exchange of fire between enemy pickets keeps death hanging in the air: a prelude. Meanwhile, soldiers in Company D face the daily task of foraging for potatoes and cabbage, gathering firewood, finding water, and cooking barely edible meals over open fires, sometimes in the rain, often in the dark. While foraging, Newton on one occasion finds fresh evidence of nearby Confederate forces, including canteens, belts, and cartridge boxes. Once, on a Sunday, he ventures back across the Ohio River and watches the local Cincinnati militia marching through the city streets. Resident soldiers, even if preparing for an imminent attack, at least get to sleep at home, in a warm bed, out of the rain.

"*E*very man under arms!"

The sudden thunderclap-command cuts through the nighttime silence. *We got up rubbing our eyes and almost expected to see the rebels coming into us.*

Company D hastily tumbles into action. Some soldiers no doubt grip their rifles with white knuckles. Company A is sent out to meet the enemy, but, strangely, the enemy has already vanished, retreating in a rush. Or maybe it was a false alarm. Nobody knows. Pulses soon settle, and Newton, as he later describes the incident for the *Reflector*, reassures the folks back home that the Huron County boys soon got back to sleep—after a few minutes of stargazing. And so it goes. A war in which enemy scouts and pickets slip through the night woods, ghostlike, produces regular false alarms, but the fear produced by false alarms is real—and, cumulatively, exhausting. On their next turn at picket duty, Newton and Company D stand guard in the woods through the night, through the following day, and all through a second straight night.

Back in camp, there is no respite from the grinding hours of readiness. Sleep is a fantasy. Another sudden loud shout breaks into the quiet darkness.

"Rally on the reverse!"

Company D rallies on the reverse—scrambling back into a defensive position—only to disperse after yet another false alarm. Phantom fighters, enemy campfires, random shots on nighttime picket duty, drilling, marching, digging potatoes, sleeping on the ground covered with a rubber blanket: this is Newton's world in September and early October 1862. Midnight alarms now belong to the ragged fabric of his everyday experience, which means that any alarm may be false or true, irrelevant or life-threatening. Such uncertainties add one more degree of not-knowing to the wartime experiences that Newton once believed would provide unreckoned value for his future life. First, he needs to survive. I wonder how he feels about his future life now.

THE GOOD SOLDIER

Reconstruction is the name applied to the period from 1865 to 1877, following Lee's surrender. Northern troops occupy the defeated South, and Northern politicians rewrite the rules of Southern life. It is a period of turmoil and unfulfilled promises. Following Lincoln's death, Republicans—the anti-slavery party—win a majority in both houses of Congress, allowing them to enact the Fourteenth Amendment guaranteeing citizenship and basic civil rights to the freed slaves. Reconstruction also requires the defeated secessionist states to remove former Confederate officers and politicians from positions of authority, which opens local and national offices to African American males, who in great numbers register to vote. The Department of War, charged with assisting freed slaves in the South, creates the Freedmen's Bureau to help educate and to empower blacks, whom slaveholders as a deliberate strategy had kept in ignorance. "Carpetbaggers" from the North descend on the South, some do-gooders, some profiteers and opportunists. Corruption proves almost inevitable.

The final withdrawal of federal forces in 1877, which brings Reconstruction to an abrupt halt, produces in the defeated South a predictable, ugly, murderous backlash. White southerners regain control of state legislatures and impose discriminatory race-based statutes (the infamous Jim Crow laws) that officially separate whites and blacks. Ku Klux Klan vigilante groups back up the Jim Crow laws with lynchings and an open campaign of terror.

Richmond lies in ruins. Union troops burn vast areas to the ground as the city falls in 1865. The capital of the Confederacy was previously a thriving center of trade and industry, home to the Tredegar Iron Works and the Richmond Laboratory. What will become of the white workers? Who will defend, educate, and find jobs for thousands of former slaves? The Freedman's Bureau can hardly do more than gesture toward possible answers, and then Reconstruction comes to an abrupt, incomplete, inglorious, and politically motivated end.

CIVIL WAR *Duet*

Richmond's Confederate monuments today stand as the direct heritage of Reconstruction and its aftermath, as white southerners reclaimed their lost power following the departure of federal forces. The monuments and the end of Reconstruction reflect the stuttering, back-and-forth, perplexing pace of national race relations ever since. In 2018 Sterling Tucker, age ninety-four, a veteran leader in the black community, offers this assessment on the occasion of Martin Luther King Jr. Day: "I've been involved in the civil rights movement since my college days, and I'm not sure I've ever been more confused than I am right now."

"If you are white," as historian and activist Rebecca Solnit observes, "you could consider that the civil war ended in 1865." A big mistake. She continues: "The blowback against Reconstruction, the rise of Jim Crow, the myriad forms of segregation and deprivation of rights and freedoms and violence against black people kept the population subjugated and punished into the present in ways that might as well be called war." Racism surges during the early twenty-first century, along with racial bias, anti-immigrant fervor, attacks on synagogues, open hostility toward Muslims, and discrimination directed at so-called "outsiders." It isn't a traditional war, or even a culture war, but an undeclared, unfinished, simmering race-based conflict that shows few signs of resolution. A con man—the archetypal shape-shifting American snake oil salesman—now occupies the White House. His political tactic for remaining in office dictates playing upon racial fears and resentments that remain in circulation precisely because the Civil War doesn't end in 1865 but generates a toxic fallout that continues to inflict damage on successive generations.

Newton Brown, if he and I bear any psychic resemblance, is no doubt focused less on politics or culture than on staying alive. My survival technique amid apparent chaos aboard the *Sea Shepherd II*? Do my job. I keep writing in my notebook as the first mate fires rounds from an AK-47 toward a Japanese driftnet ship. I'm doing my writer's job. Keep the ink flowing across the page. It seems the best course available—short of primal magic—in order not to die.

*C*incinnati continues to prepare for the anticipated Confederate attack. The local militia, which Newton watches one Sunday as they drill, is no match for the Confederate army massing across the Ohio River. Their nickname—the Squirrel Hunters—bears witness both to their antiquated firearms and to their part-time status. The professional defense of Cincinnati thus falls, among others, to the 101st Ohio Regiment, rank amateurs, but at least full-time soldiers with genuine guns, uniforms, and knapsacks. On September 9, Company D takes up positions in Kentucky about a half mile from their temporary base, Camp Stem. Their specific mission is to defend the artillery batteries defending Fort Mitchel, a crucial link in a chain of seven forts designed and built specifically to defend the port city of Cincinnati.

General Ormsby M. Mitchel—multitalented professor, attorney, surveyor, publisher, and astronomer—designs the seven forts, and Fort Mitchel bears his name. Newton's job (the task assigned to Company D) is to man the trenches that surround the fort, called rifle pits. The rifle pits at Fort Mitchel, as Newton writes, are *no trifling affair*. He adds, awed, that they take up *a circuit of many miles*.

I find it hard to imagine what he is seeing, so I'm pleased to find a contemporary engraving (Figure 7) that shows Fort Mitchel atop a Kentucky hillside broad enough to accommodate miles of surrounding rifle pits.

Newton no doubt recognizes that their position exposes the entire company to the first wave of any Confederate infantry assault on Fort Mitchel, and an assault on Fort Mitchel is necessary if the Rebels plan to take Cincinnati.

Who digs the rifle pits? Not Newton, not Company D. The rifle trenches and defensive earthworks at Fort Mitchel are the recent work of some one thousand African Americans. Known as the Black Brigade, they are not soldiers but residents of Cincinnati, and they have responded to the less-than-catchy rallying cry from General Lew Wallace, "Civilians for labor, soldiers for battle." The black volunteers respond so quickly that Cincinnati officials, caught by surprise, panic at seeing a throng of black men bearing picks and shovels. The police soon arrive, and what follows is a typical violent, race-based police roundup. General Wallace later issues both an apology and a commendation to the Black Brigade. Their work well done, they fade into the remote history of Cincinnati and into the untold story of African American contributions to the Civil War.

Thursday, the enemy were to be seen in large numbers some two miles from here.

Newton and the Company D soldiers in the rifle pits remain on high alert, resting with rifles beside them and cartridge boxes strapped to their chests. Sounds of gunshots get Newton's attention. *The pickets fired all day.* It is starting to feel like war. Already tell-tale signs point to heavy combat ahead. Prisoners are brought in. Enemy soldiers are killed. *Our side,* Newton adds, also loses *a few men.* His words seem oddly casual, as if a few losses now count as an acceptable exchange in the increasingly active skirmishes preliminary to the massed combat of opposing armies.

Death—not personified on a biblical pale horse but embodied in ashen-grey human corpses—is becoming an everyday companion.

The heavy skirmishing continues around Fort Mitchel. Then, on September 12, the entire Regiment is ordered back to Camp Stem, some half-dozen miles from Fort Mitchel. Why? Awaiting orders, the Huron County boys build a communal lean-to covered with brush, which they name (with a mixture of state pride and architectural irony) Buckeye Hall. A steady rain no doubt hastens its construction—and perhaps also dampens Rebel plans for an assault. Unknowns proliferate. Foremost among the cloud cover of unknowing? Mysteriously, the very large Confederate force gathered with the apparent goal of taking Cincinnati simply melts away.

The departure of the Confederate forces around Cincinnati remains among the stranger wartime puzzles. Newton knows nothing of the military chess game leading to this inexplicable anticlimax. Company D has done its job. Cincinnati is saved!

"Every white person should read this book." I make this unusual race-based statement—despite my skepticism about the idea of race—as I explain to several close friends the intense discomfort I experience while reading *Underground Railroad* (2016). Written by African American novelist Colson Whitehead, it hasn't yet won both a Pulitzer Prize and a National Book Award when canny librarians at Virginia Commonwealth University sign up the author for a lecture. I am in the audience as Whitehead begins his talk, and it seems an odd beginning, devoted mainly to a long comic riff on his life as a writer in now-hip Brooklyn. He knows what he's doing. When he turns to read from his book, the mood turns dark and bleak. Although the book is a *tour de force* of magical realism, Whitehead forces his readers—if they persist—to experience slavery not as a system (historical, economic, social, or agrarian) but as a sequence of unspeakable atrocities. The horrifying details, even lightly fictionalized, are hard to stomach.

What makes the novel more bearable than a sequence of atrocities is Whitehead's childhood fantasy that the underground railroad consists of actual trains running in tunnels like a private subway for runaway slaves. Freedom on Whitehead's fantasy railroad, however, proves elusive or impossible, as slaveholders punish captured runaways with brutal torture. I feel sick as I understand how far slavery in America involved whites beating, raping, burning, killing, and dismembering blacks.

Newton is focused on fighting against the Confederate army, but he probably knows that the fight extends to laws supporting slavery that have the imprimatur of the United States Congress. The Fugitive Slave Act of 1850 imposes penalties on anyone who aids or abets runaway slaves. It requires that runaway slaves be returned to their rightful owners. Thus its provisions enlist all Americans in tacit support of slavery, and even free states such as Ohio are open to legal invasion by slave-catching bounty hunters. In *Underground Railroad*, these long-ago historical legalities and injustices suddenly take on flesh-and-blood terror. They implicate every citizen, past and future, in an appalling racist system in which—as Whitehead takes us beyond political or economic abstractions—black slaves are lashed to the bone, run down by bloodhounds, lynched, and (in a strategy to multiply terror) left hanging from trees.

"Much has been said about American slavery," Thoreau writes in 1854, "but I think that we do not even yet realize what slavery is." Newton may have read this line from Thoreau's essay "Slavery in Massachusetts." I too had not yet realized what slavery is—before reading *Underground Railroad*. I am learning now. I am learning too, firsthand, about the dangers of government-sanctioned racism, whether expressed in presidential rhetoric or in unjust laws. Thoreau's attack on the Fugitive Slave Law begins with a measured sentence that still resonates profoundly today: "I wish my countrymen to consider, that whatever the human law may be, neither an individual nor a nation can ever commit the least act of injustice against the obscurest individual without having to pay the penalty for it."

Late September finds Newton and Company D on the move once again in Kentucky, heading toward another hotspot, Louisville. Louisville is the real prize sought by the massed Confederate forces under Generals Braxton Bragg and Edmund Kirby Smith, as some historians believe. The apparent assault on Cincinnati, in this scenario, is a shrewd diversionary tactic. Louisville is no sleepy backwater town on the Ohio River. It is a major stronghold for Union forces, crucial in keeping the entire state of Kentucky in the Union, and a center for military planning, supplies, and transportation, especially in the Western theater. Lewis Day rightly calls it "the great military center of the West."

The journey begins with a dusty early-morning march from Camp Stem to the Cincinnati railroad depot. Trains, as powerful symbols of nineteenth-century industrial progress, come in several flavors. Newton's ride begins aboard a passenger train, but the comfort level drops precipitously as Company D soon shifts to no-frills, bone-rattling cattle cars. The freight train jolts past several Union armies camped along the tracks: the 19th Michigan and the 83rd Indiana. The 101st Ohio Regiment is on its way to merge with a vast patchwork Union army. The three steamboats they pass, loaded with soldiers, get only a passing comment. It is not the oddest circumstance. Once disembarked from their cattle cars and back on foot, Company D marches right past Louisville and presses onward for another two hours toward the town of Jeffersonville.

It has been a long, weary, pounding day of travel, by rail and on foot. When they finally stop for the night, the exhausted soldiers spread their blankets on the ground. Readers of the *Reflector* might admire the stoical account. "We made the best of it, as good soldiers should."

I'm confused. The content is clear enough, but the writer, for several reasons, doesn't sound like Newton. I remain puzzled for several months, until I realize that the author isn't Newton but rather a fellow soldier from Company D, Ira Beman Read. "Beeman," as everyone calls him, is the son of a respected Norwalk physician, Albert N. Read. Newton explains in a letter that Beman's account of the journey to Jeffersonville must have arrived at the *Reflector* before his similar description. If he feels scooped, however, Newton gives no sign of rancor. He and Beman evidently don't discuss their submissions. Beman, a sergeant, outranks Newton and has already graduated from college. In any case, they both contribute two published dispatches to the *Reflector* during September. Thereafter, accounts from Company D in the *Reflector* are written by Beman Read, who signs them with the letter *B*. After September 1862, with only one much later exception, Newton's accounts (always signed *JNB*) simply stop.

Something feels amiss. It is Beman who describes the six-mile march from Camp Stem to the Cincinnati train depot, followed by the two-stage railroad transport and long march to Jeffersonville. His account includes a minor comic incident—my initial point of bafflement—when their cattle car stops near a water tank. The steam-driven engine needs to take on water, and as the refilling proceeds a four-inch-diameter waterspout accidentally breaks loose. The account in the *Reflector* continues: "Our friend Newton was thoroughly washed, but took it as philosophically as the occasion admitted."

Our friend Newton? Would a real friend tell everyone in Huron County and beyond that Newton Brown, by name, got soaked from an errant water hose? Is there a concealed backstory? I wonder if these two Huron County boys, Beman and Newton, are not only rival journalists but also silent rivals for the hand of Hattie Sparhawk. Beman in his reports never again singles out a soldier by name. He makes no efforts at humor. Right now, I am not much liking Beman Read.

Beman needs some help from Newton as a writer, since the bulk of his account of the Jeffersonville journey enumerates all the small towns they pass on the train. He highlights a beautiful flagpole and reports on some "awful bitter peach pies." The rather tedious account culminates with what he calls the most attractive sight encountered on their journey: "a very pretty lady." She is dressed in pink, Beman adds, "waving what I thought was a large bunch of red, white, and blue ribbons." I tip my hat to Beman for journalistic integrity: he does not state that she *actually* waved the patriotic ribbons—only that he "thought" she did. Did he invent the tricolor ribbons as a special effect? I wonder only because he includes some entirely gratuitous remarks about his distinguished father and then concludes—here I un-tip my hat—by sucking up to the editor: "I spent a pleasant hour last evening looking over a *Reflector*. Let 'em come."

All politics is local, as the saying goes, and for a soldier all wars are also local. War is less about grand alliances and winning strategies than about the fight to take a particular hill or to defend a specific patch of ground. The Civil War, from a soldier's perspective, involves open fields, muddy roads, stone fences, swollen streams, rain-soaked woods, and dry gunpowder. For Newton, the localness of war means ponds, barnyards, and campfires. The ultimate resolution of this great national struggle cannot be achieved without all-day marches through towns whose names nobody remembers. Even when Newton crosses from Ohio into Kentucky, the political fiction of state lines gets translated into the local facts of enemy territory. In the era before cyberspace and military satellites, the Civil War remains a series of local battlefield encounters that always occur (or *take place*) somewhere in particular. It is time to look at a map (Figure 8).

Kentucky is the central prize.

This map is designed to show the area proximate to Confederate General Bragg's invasion of Kentucky in 1862, and I've added dark ovals to indicate key locales on Newton's journey. The top oval highlights Cincinnati as the southernmost city in the free state of Ohio and a gateway to Kentucky. In Kentucky, Louisville and Perryville will also prove important in Newton's progress, as will Nashville in neighboring Tennessee. Tennessee when the war starts is staunchly pro-Union, but also—at the local level—sharply divided. It is the last southern state to secede, after a close vote, and (as a sure mark of its importance and divisions) more battles are fought in Tennessee during the Civil War than in any state except Virginia.

The 101st Regiment will fight in several decisive battles in Tennessee and conclude its deployment at war's end somewhere—to the bottom right of the map—in the mountains of North Carolina. These locales represent, starting in 1862, the center of Newton Brown's world—but it is a world destined to expand in ways he is not yet prepared to understand.

THE GOOD SOLDIER

"The history of the world," writes the nineteenth-century sage Thomas Carlyle, "is but the biography of great men." Maybe so. War occasionally raises individuals to heroic stature, and Grant, in altering the course of American history, perhaps altered the history of the world. The Civil War also transforms a previously obscure Illinois state politician into America's greatest president. There is surely room for the "great man" version of history, although the subgenre is notably lacking in "great woman" narratives. As a corrective to heroic narratives of every gender, not as a replacement or damning critique, I am more interested in lives that elude the hyper-magnification of so-called greatness and heroism. History needs to include people whose lives do not approach heroic stature or call for the construction of horseback monuments.

Newton reports that someone has stolen his canteen. The loss of a canteen is no trivial matter, considering long marches, scarce water, and the dangers of dehydration. Theft is a surprising problem in the camps. George Drake writes that someone steals his "post folder" with "all its contents." His stolen property includes, I assume, the letters he has saved: a soldier's lifeline. A brief entry in the *Reflector* on the death of one Edwin W. Cunningham, who fought with the 101st Ohio Regiment, praises him for avoiding "those petty acts of pilfering which are so common among soldiers." This is a strangely negative point of praise—Cunningham was *not* a petty thief—but it raises questions usually unaddressed in histories of the Civil War. What does it take to maintain your values in camps where fellow soldiers routinely steal from their comrades in arms?

I've got so that I don't care much what happens to what little I have with me, only so that I preserve my integrity, my health, & do the work appointed me.

A canteen and a water hose have mute stories to tell. Newton's canteen provides him with an occasion for acknowledging his changed outlook. Even a stolen canteen, it appears, may come to possess unreckoned value. Pilfering and death or the fear of death make an odd couple, but together they help to define the outlines of Newton's new everyday life. They also contribute to a clarification of what truly matters. Integrity, health, and duty. This trio—a survival kit of values—doesn't amount to a comprehensive virtue-based ethics, but it identifies a set of personal priorities that serve Newton as guiding principles in a setting where principles and values seem hard to come by.

Writing is an action that Newton and I implicitly infuse with value, even if he never thinks of himself as a writer. It took me a long time before I felt willing to take the leap of calling myself a writer. Writers for me meant Shakespeare, Milton, and Melville. A linguistic self-deception—finding the noun hidden within a verb—finally let me join the circle. What do you call someone who drives a truck? A truck driver. What do you call someone who sings? A singer. What do you call someone who writes? Writers, in this linguistic dance, are not necessarily giants of world literature—the writer as hero—but people who perform the action of writing. Newton, although he sees his future in the church, always seems to be writing. As a first-year college student he writes an essay on the early history of Ripley that appears in print while he is in uniform. His account offers no hint of the backwoods "Indian hating" that Ohio writer James Hall describes in *Legends of the West* (1832). Newton even includes two long anecdotes about settlers whose fear of Indians proves baseless: little parables about the error of racial stereotypes.

Newton's preference as a writer lies, as it does for Emerson, less with the itinerant local Indians—who embodied Thoreau's virtue of wildness—than with the spiritualized labor that transforms a pristine wilderness into productive farms. "What is a farm," Emerson asks in *Nature* (1836), "but a mute gospel?" Newton's father, a farmer and a religious man, might agree with this assertion couched as a rhetorical question. Emerson continues: "The chaff and the wheat, weeds and plants, blight, rain, insects, sun, —it is a sacred emblem from the first furrow of spring to the last stack which the snow of winter overtakes in the fields."

What Newton and Emerson seem to lack as writers—a fault I own—is an element of playfulness. "A man is fed," writes Emerson in his high-serious vein, "not that he may be fed, but that he may work." Work and duty (redefined as spiritual activities and ultimate values) may blind Newton to more lighthearted pursuits, much as Emerson fails to see the humor when he portrays himself as a transparent eyeball. Seriousness, unleavened by play, can prove a serious limitation. I suspect that Newton's unpublished account of the Jeffersonville train ride fails to mention the "pretty lady" in a pink dress waving red, white, and blue ribbons. OK. I apologize to Beman Read and his descendants. Newton may have known contemporary Victorian proponents of high seriousness such as Matthew Arnold and Thomas Carlyle, but he failed to give equal weight to their American contemporaries, as when Thoreau goes fishing and when Whitman loafs and invites his soul, although Thoreau and Whitman (in their different ways) are hardly un-serious writers. Beman as an amateur journalist may have already learned or known instinctively what many serious writers know: the valuable secret of letting go.

We are learning something about marching. Newton's dry remark conveys an ironic commentary on the limits of his military education. The statement, in a letter home on September 27, 1862, demonstrates his penchant for understatement, as the letter describes yet another six-mile march, followed by a 3:00 a.m. call to take up positions in line of battle, which means hours of standing in place. *It was harder than marching to stand with knapsack on.*

His understated, subdued tone in late September may reflect a sense that a major battle is imminent. Lewis Day dispenses with understatement. He describes the 101st Regiment as "rolling onward to the point at which the shock of contending armies would soon be felt." The Ohio cavalry has arrived, Newton writes, four hundred strong. He explains that the cavalry has lost one man killed and one man wounded—*in an engagement with 2,000 enemy*! This is the only nearby Confederate force about which he has received even semi-reliable information, and the enemy force is twice the size of the 101st Regiment. Something significant has changed on the ground.

We have an enormous army here. I cannot write more now for I must hurry off to picket duty.

Colonel Leander Stem writes to his wife on the last day of September. A commander about to lead his thousand-man regiment into combat has little time for domestic details. Stem's days are occupied with meeting generals, planning strategy, and deploying troops. There is no time to reflect on the law practice he abruptly left behind. A contemporary portrait (Figure 9) depicts him with an intense gaze, thoughtful and introspective, looking less like a Civil War commander than like a dark Romantic poet.

Colonel Stem in fact has almost no military experience. He worries that his inexperience exposes him to the back-stabbing maneuvers of military rivals who covet his status and position.

He knows that something big is coming. He knows too that his wife will read his letter to the assembled family circle, and he closes on a note that any anxious, lonely foot soldier—with a major battle looming—would surely recognize: "I am disappointed at not getting any letter from home since here. Why don't you all write?"

CIVIL WAR *Duet*

OCTOBER 1862: PERRYVILLE

"Strike tents!"

The order comes just as the Huron County boys—returned from Jeffersonville—are settling in for the night. The only tents are reserved for officers, so perhaps Newton is bedding down in Buckeye Hall, but not for long. By 10:00 p.m. Company D is on the road again, in darkness, marching the familiar six miles to Cincinnati. For long stretches, the immediate adversary has been boredom. "A little too much guard duty to suit us," remarks one of Newton's fellow soldiers, adding that his duties once consisted entirely in guarding an officer's corn crib.

The nighttime order to strike tents carries an urgent feel, unlike the now-familiar false alarms. Now they are moving on, in the dark, as if they are at last marching into battle. Enemy pickets harass them soon after they leave. Colonel Stem counters by sending out scouts, well-armed. Dawn is breaking as the 101st Infantry boards a passenger train, whose slow pace does not prevent bone-jolts worthy of a cattle car.

"The departure of our army on that beautiful first day of October 1862, must have been a grand sight," Lewis Day writes, ignoring a few inconvenient facts while creating an image no doubt true to the mood of the day. "In five magnificent columns it poured southward for the express purpose of giving battle to an army equal in size and almost within hearing distance."

The vision is grand only in hindsight. The 101st Infantry, after marching six miles in darkness followed by a jolting daylight train ride, then disembarks to march another ten miles, across fields, over fences, and through woods. Newton soldiers on. Some of the Huron County boys don't straggle into camp until nearly midnight. No matter. The march resumes early the next morning. The monthlong encampment in Kentucky has added cumbersome acquisitions. Alonzo Bishop, another Company D marcher, writes that his fellow soldiers during their first few weeks have acquired "numerous trinkets": "We resembled the old time pack peddler with knapsacks bulging from every angle, and frying pans, kettles and a little of everything tied not only to our knapsacks, but even to our belts and even to our coat buttons."

Every few miles soldiers discard unnecessary items until the roadside, as Bishop puts it, "looked like a dump pile." Even Colonel Stem jettisons useless gear. A moving roadside dump doesn't quite match Lewis Day's description of "a grand sight." The large jumble of discarded blankets and knapsacks needs to be gathered up and sent on to Louisville for storage. Who gets chosen to transport it? Beman Read. Hard-pressed, he settles on a four-horse mule wagon, driven, he writes, by "a hump-backed darkey." Beman deposits the cast-off military dump in Louisville with the Sanitary Commission, perhaps relying on his father's wartime connections. The trip to Louisville, however, proves far less hazardous than finding his way back. "It is no easy matter to find a regiment on the march," he informs the *Reflector*, "especially when there are other divisions around." With Union and Confederate forces assembling from all directions, Sergeant Read needs to make certain that he finds his way back to the right army.

The next day, unforgettable, begins at 2:00 a.m. The call goes out to cook breakfast and to get ready to march. Two hours later Company D is on the road again, including Beman Read, who has found his way back. Early October in Kentucky can feel like mid-summer. "It was a very warm day," Beman tells the *Reflector*, "and we had great difficulty in getting any water at all." Not just water. "Good water was entirely out of the question."

It is the hardest march that Company D has made, Beman explains, as they march for an entire day, with no rest. Exhausted soldiers drop by the roadside under the merciless sun. A severe drought has coated the limestone-covered roads with thick choking lime dust. Newton's throat is parched, his legs ache, and his feet swell with blisters. Onward they march, from predawn until long after sunset, for thirty-two grueling miles, and by evening Company D has dropped to just thirty men. Some stragglers are never heard from again.

Dinner late that night means foraging in the dark. Newton settles for a watery broth of potatoes, onions, and beets.

"Our suffering was intense," Lewis Day sums up. *Suffering* is the operative word, perhaps too easy to discount. I had imagined that suffering in the Civil War is a battlefield phenomenon, but the noncombat lives of Union and Confederate soldiers make suffering a steady companion. Day continues his account: "All in all, it was probably as severe a day's marching as the Regiment ever experienced." Newton, who rarely complains, writes that the notorious march *did come near killing me*.

The intense suffering of their long march through Kentucky, however, is a prelude to the horrors that Newton witnesses soon after they arrive somewhere near the small, rural town of Perryville. Killing is no longer a metaphor.

Neither racism nor slavery ends with the Emancipation Proclamation, nor with the Thirteenth Amendment, nor with the Confederate surrender. Although today we sanitize our speech with polite references to the "n-word," our brains fill in the blank. Respectable patients on dementia wards who lose prefrontal controls sometimes spew vile racist slurs, suggesting how far even apparently decent people are infected. Infection is a metaphor, but apt. Once, in the 1990s, while a visiting professor, I learn that a faculty member venerated for his commitment to civil rights and racial justice is about to retire. The student paper sends a reporter to interview him. After the usual questions about his lifelong passion, the reporter asks why so few black students take his courses. "You must understand," he replies, "these are very hard courses."

The metaphor of infection is not meant to excuse conscious or nonconscious acts of racism. My point is that racism afflicts all Americans. The infection is passed down to subsequent generations like a virus transmitted from parent to child. Why does Moses decide that the Israelites need to wander in the desert for forty years? Why forty years instead of five or fifty? My answer concerns metaphoric infection. Moses knows it will take at least an entire new generation—children born outside of Egyptian captivity—for Jews to overcome their slave mentality. Slavery confines the body, but its fundamental damage plays out in the mind and the spirit. Nor is it only the oppressed who are damaged. The infection of slavery damages the oppressors. It poisons slaveholders as well as slaves. "I can testify from my own experience and observation," writes Harriet Jacobs in her autobiographical *Incidents in the Life of a Slave Girl* (1861), "that slavery is a curse to the whites as well as to the blacks. It makes the white fathers cruel and sensual; the sons violent and licentious; it contaminates the daughters, and makes the wives wretched."

There is good reason to take seriously Jacobs's description of slavery as a curse and a contamination, evoking the feverish atmosphere of a tale by Edgar Allan Poe. Slavery exposes a diseased, inflamed, malformed heart within the celebrated American Adam. A mythic figure, the American Adam represents the nineteenth-century vision of a New Man (yes, male) appropriate to the vast, untrammeled continent and sublime landscape that writers and painters compare to the Garden of Eden: a natural paradise, free from the sins of Old Europe, where humankind reclaims its original Innocence. Emerson, Thoreau, and

Whitman all at moments embrace the myth of American innocence and natural goodness. The Civil War unravels the myth but never quite manages to kill it. The vision of America as a biblical shining city on a hill reappears throughout the succeeding years, but it also never erases an uneasy recognition that this vibrant, boundless, race-torn nation is, like the hero of a gothic novel, simultaneously—choose your metaphor—cursed, contaminated, and infected.

The American Adam is of course white. So are the vast majority of writers and painters who manufacture the mythic narrative of national innocence. They conceal or fail to grasp how the New World is not only infected by slavery but also cursed by the accompanying racist genocide against native peoples. Colson Whitehead's postmodern alternative to the nineteenth-century narrative of national innocence is a magical-realist horror story, but even Whitehead fails to convey how slavery in America infects the oppressors as well as the oppressed—and all of their descendants. If almost no one is free from the infection of slavery, then freedom for all Americans is compromised—until, as a nation, we can (once and for all) finish the Civil War.

Dearest Friends. It brings tears into my eyes to read your letters. Don't think I'm homesick but distance brings my heart nearer to yours.

Tears. Newton in mid-October 1862 may be using a figure of speech—but perhaps not. He strikes me as big-hearted, and I too have a sentimental side. You can expect me to choke up at schmaltzy films. The tendency to dismiss or denigrate emotion as unreliable, feminine, and downright dangerous is a cultural prejudice worth questioning. Tears are a basic biological endowment. Our feelings can certainly get us into trouble—so can reason—but at times they prove an indispensable resource. In *Uncle Tom's Cabin* (1852), Harriet Beecher Stowe deploys the emotional power of the sentimental novel in order to inspire widespread opposition to slavery. The novel is wildly popular. The two-volume edition sells fifty thousand copies in its first six months, and six months later it reaches an astounding quarter-million copies sold.

Slavery in *Uncle Tom's Cabin* can't be distanced by readers as a faraway practice or as an issue of states' rights. You feel the pathos as bloodhounds close in upon an escaping black mother who cradles her child in her arms, trapped at the edge of an icy river. Stage versions—multiplying the impact of the novel—add the emotional power of live performance. Emotions are a necessary spark for significant social action. On a visit to Washington ten years after publication of *Uncle Tom's Cabin*, Stowe meets Lincoln at the White House. He takes her hand and—reportedly, since the account comes from her daughter—asks the now-famous question, "Is this the little woman who made the great war?"

Colonel Stem's cautionary address at Camp Monroeville is coldly reasonable, almost arithmetical—"Some shall not return"—but arithmetic alone does not always carry persuasion. I suspect that most soldiers who hear Stem's address believe they are among the exceptional ones who will return. Most people lay their bets as their emotions dictate, and our emotions also tell us when to change our bets. "You should hear the surmises and plans made by the boys here in camp," Beman Read writes from Kentucky to the *Reflector*. "A while ago some of them were going to be at home New Year's, but I guess they have given that up."

The geopolitical fault lines that make a quick homecoming improbable are clear in a map published in 1856. Congress in 1782 had adopted the phrase *E Pluribus Unum* as the motto appearing on the official Seal of the United States, but the split between northern and southern states sends a lateral fracture across the eastern half of the country that exposes the One-From-Many slogan as wishful thinking (Figure 10).

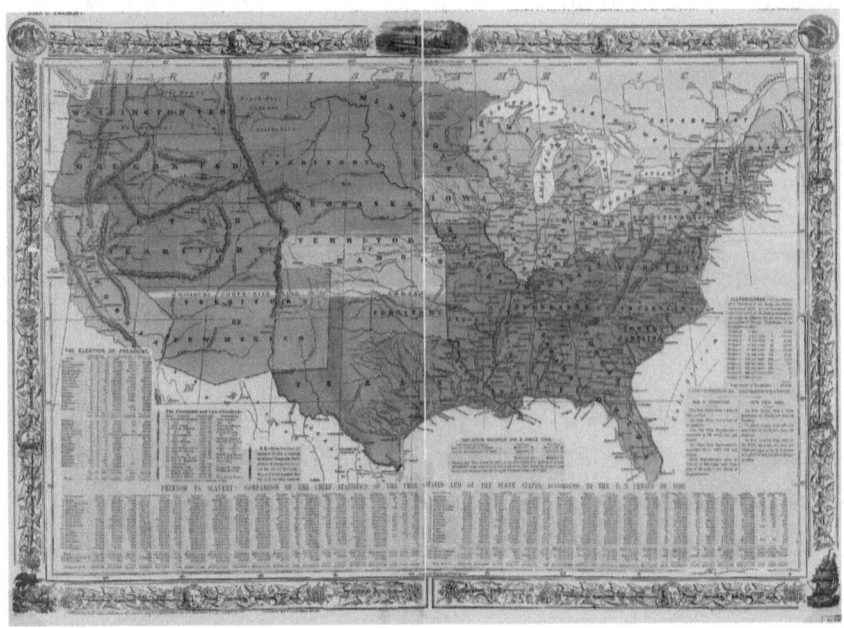

The Many in their conflict over slavery threaten to turn the young country into the permanently Dis-United States. The wide-open, non-state western territories promise still more division and fresh opportunities for discord. Which side—slave or free—will the fledgling new states join?

The blank space at the center of the map is the territory of Kansas, like a snub-nosed pistol pointed west. Its undecided fate, whether to enter the Union as slave or free, reflects the split condition of the national body politic. It also points toward a paradox inherent in emotion. The same power of feeling that Stowe taps into, deploying the resources of the sentimental novel to change hearts and minds, also fuels the near-religious and impassioned conversion that propels John Brown (in his hatred of slavery) to plan a violent and bloody race war. Stowe and Brown reflect two views of emotion and two opposed visions of America.

THE GOOD SOLDIER

Democracy can be as volatile and repressive as tyranny, which is one reason why Plato in the *Republic* believed that democracies—freedom run wild in a paradoxical inverse servitude—will lead directly to tyrannies. Congress in 1854 grants Kansas the right to determine its status by democratic popular vote. In leaving the fate of Kansas to a popular vote, however, Congress in its wisdom might as well have added the legal postscript: "Let the bloodshed begin...."

Almost on cue, John Brown—earlier converted to the abolitionist cause in something close to an epiphany—arrives in the Kansas territory in 1855. His sons, already living there, have reported fears concerning pro-slavery militants, and their fears are well founded. In 1856, a pro-slavery mob from Missouri—led by a local sheriff—crosses into Kansas, invades the town of Lawrence, and burns down the Free State Hotel. Brown has no sympathy for pacifists, and abolitionists who promote nonviolent change, such as William Lloyd Garrison, strike him as fainthearted. "These men are all talk," Brown complains. "What we need is action—action!"

Stowe deals in sentiment, and Brown deals in blood. Action means hacking to death with broadswords five pro-slavery settlers. Known as the Pottawatomie Massacre, it simply generates predictable pro-slavery retaliations. As the bloody acts of vengeance escalate, Kansas quickly earns its popular nickname, "Bleeding" Kansas.

Dear Reflector. Since I last wrote you, we Huron County boys have been experiencing a good deal in a short time. We have realized all that precedes a battle: all the marching to and fro; all the expectation and preparation; but have not yet taken part in the fight.

Lewis Day concurs. "Although we were nearing the crisis," he writes, "although the time at which the two great armies were to come into deadly conflict had almost arrived, yet our daily camp life went right along as though nothing was expected." Readers in Ohio might be excused for thinking that life in the 101st Infantry could be summarized as camps, train rides, marches, drills, and picket duty. Your worst experience, putting aside the memory of a brutal twenty-four-hour march, might be getting soaked by a runaway waterhose. The preparations, the false alarms, the long hours standing guard at your post in the woods holding a heavy rifle and strapped into a heavy knapsack? All this is about to change, although not without a few close calls to rachet up the tension.

At 3 o'clock Wednesday morning the alarm was given and the pickets were ordered to rally. Our cavalry had discovered the enemy advancing in force some 6 miles from here on the pike. —This was not deemed sufficient cause for rallying, so we returned to our posts.

Kansas enters the Union as a free state in January 1861, still bleeding. Its entry inflames more discord. Conflict rages in Kansas throughout the war, with surplus atrocities. In 1863, pro-slavery forces in Kansas sack and burn the unlucky town of Lawrence, killing more than one hundred people. Many combatants in Kansas come, like John Brown, from elsewhere, and bloodshed seems inescapable in a twilight zone where only an invisible state line separates Missouri pro-slavery partisans from Kansas anti-slavery partisans. Passions run hot, and the violence threatens to unleash chaos. Before the question of statehood is decided, however, the 1860 election of Lincoln as president—on an anti-slavery Republican platform—finally sweeps not only Kansas but the entire divided nation into battle. In 1861, seven slaveholding states—South Carolina, Mississippi, Florida, Alabama, Georgia, Louisiana, and Texas—secede from the Union and create the Confederate States of America. Ultimately eleven southern states secede.

During his first year at Oberlin College, Newton is watching the nation unravel, which propels his enlistment in the late summer of 1862. Ohio, while a free state, shares its southern border with Kentucky, and Kentucky remains problematic. Split between pro-slavery and anti-slavery forces, Kentucky also seeks to avoid the self-inflicted damage inescapable after choosing sides, so, in an unresolvable impasse, it declares neutrality. This declaration does not prevent Confederate generals Bragg, Longstreet, Davis, Lee, and Hood from coveting Kentucky as a prize of war, and a Confederate invasion of Kentucky in the fall of 1862 disrupts its fig-leaf fiction of neutrality. Kentucky then officially sides with the Union, although this official pronouncement (another time-serving move) does nothing to lessen the unofficial, passionate divisions within towns and homes.

Lincoln—born and raised in Kentucky—understands the importance of holding his native state for the Union. Newton and the Huron County boys, if they didn't know already, are learning fast about the strategic political and military importance of their confused neighbor state as they march steadily southward during the early autumn of 1862, dodging sharpshooters and standing picket duty, in ever-rising anticipation of a major battle just ahead.

I grow up in Delaware during the 1950s mostly oblivious to its Civil War history. Turmoil in Delaware makes Kentucky seem like a land of peace and reason. A slave state, Delaware nonetheless votes (on January 3, 1861) to remain in the Union. One reason why: 90 percent of the state's black population is free by 1860. Proximity to Philadelphia—a Quaker stronghold opposed to slavery—no doubt prompts many slaveholders in northern Delaware to free their slaves. Delaware, however, is divided between one northern county and two southern counties, and the sympathies in rural southern Delaware lean toward slavery. You might think that Wilmington, my northern Delaware hometown, would be a center of liberal attitudes and practices regarding race. You would be mistaken. I do not have even one black classmate during my four years, from 1956 to 1960, at Mount Pleasant Senior High.

Jim Crow racism spreads northward into areas that officially or unofficially opposed slavery, and it thrives there. The 1954 landmark Supreme Court decision in *Brown v. Board of Education*, which declares segregated school systems unconstitutional, has no immediate effect in Delaware. It takes decades of negotiation among state leaders—and considerable litigation—to desegregate Wilmington public schools. The only black person I see on a semi-regular basis is the woman who helps clean our house. We refer to her, in then-polite usage, as a "colored lady"—while not really thinking of ourselves as white. We just *are*. Today I can see what I didn't see then. *Being-white*, in its many practical and philosophical senses, means being white without *thinking about* being-white.

Whiteness also means being free without thinking (much or at all) about freedom, especially as its limits define an invisible circumference around the black community. It is a circumference that in the 1950s extends to drinking fountains and rest rooms and seats in the back of the bus. The Latin word for freedom is *libertas*—sharing the same root as the political term *liberal*—personified in Roman times as a goddess akin to the torch-wielding figure on the Statue of Liberty. *Libertas* in ancient Rome is what distinguishes the citizen from the

THE GOOD SOLDIER

slave. Its freedoms are bestowed by the state and extend throughout the sphere of civil life: "liberal arts" refers originally to the education befitting a free male citizen. (Women in ancient Rome, like slaves, are not citizens.) As concepts and as social practices, liberty and freedom develop in a symbiotic relation with slavery. Slavery means not-free, and freedom means not-enslaved.

The Civil War, in ending slavery, means that Americans must rethink freedom as something other than the opposite of slavery. The ancient Roman binary opposition of slave and citizen no longer holds, and the inhabitants of the new democratic republic must come to a new understanding of what it means to be free. Freedom, so often invoked as a core American value, turns out to be a concept still in quest of a full understanding.

Northern Delaware is not alone as a locale where, in the 1950s and beyond, freedom and race prove incompatible for blacks. In 1960, my entering class in Hamilton College—a small men's liberal arts school in remote upstate New York—includes one black student. Elite American colleges and universities manage for decades to champion a liberal education while excluding blacks, Jews, women, and other minority groups secretly defined as Other. I'm grateful for the college education that I received from dedicated teachers who chose to spend their weekends correcting first-year student compositions, but this fine liberal education came, for me, at the cost of a social and racial myopia that was widely shared inside and outside the classroom.

Company D, with no time for reflections on freedom or liberal education, is preparing for battle. I try to imagine what Newton feels. Does he defuse his anxieties and steady his nerves by a focus on

CIVIL WAR *Duet*

doing his job? Duty includes its own myopia. The immense loss of life as two great armies crash together in rural Kentucky will decide nothing. Freedom is not conferred by a flag or by battlefield acts of valor. The endless resilience of racism makes a tactical military success—no matter how brave the soldiers or how costly their sacrifice—ring hollow. The "grand sight" of two magnificent armies massing for mortal combat might have struck devout Quakers such as William Penn—who understood freedom as individual "liberty of conscience" to follow the inner light of our direct personal awareness of God—as little more than a bloody pantomime.

"Something is happening here / But you don't know what it is / Do you, Mister Jones?" There is much I am seeing that, while seeing, I apparently don't see. Bob Dylan's lines from "Ballad of a Thin Man" (1965) capture the mood of the next five years that pass in a blur of uncomprehending murderous turmoil. It is a period when a media-christened generation gap ("Don't trust anyone over thirty") divides not only young from old but also hip from square, cool from un-cool, liberal from conservative, and radical anti-war protestor from God-fearing, flag-waving American patriot.

Mr. Jones and I, while not entirely clueless, nonetheless register only dimly the 1965 murder of Malcolm X. In another act of American self-creation, Malcolm Little replaces his surname with the mysterious letter *X*, signifying his rejection of the slaveholding past when plantation owners named their human property. Renamed Malcom X, he makes the transition from convict to influential leader in the black-separatist Nation of Islam and, after his 1964 break with the movement, to a controversial career as a Muslim minister, human rights activist, and radical spokesman for the black power movement. The internal politics of black liberation brews a plot against Malcolm's life, but within months of his murder *The Autobiography of Malcolm X* (1965) appears—a powerful conversion narrative co-authored by journalist Alex Haley. It quickly serves for many white readers as a primer on the new black understanding of freedom.

African American self-fashioning—in direct resistance to the historical repression of black males and to white stereotypes of blackness—soon receives a far more visible icon in the charismatic heavyweight boxing champion, Cassius Marcellus Clay. Like his mentor, friend, and religious guide Malcolm X, Clay in 1964 drops what he calls his slave name. With the national spotlight following every move, he declares that he is a convert to Islam with a new name and a new identity. "I am Muhammad Ali, a free name—it means beloved of God," he asserts, "and I insist people use it when people speak to me." Eventually, all the Joneses and all the media in America and elsewhere learn to call him Ali. More than a name was at stake.

Ali's later break with Malcolm X only helps to secure his reputation as an independent, outspoken, self-made man. Black, handsome, athletic, fast-talking, he fearlessly *tells it like it is* (in a favorite cliché of the time). As the Vietnam War heats up, he defies the call from his local draft board, on religious grounds. Stripped of his heavyweight title, banned from boxing for three years, fined ten thousand dollars, and sentenced to five years' imprisonment, he shrewdly identifies the racism implicit both in American life and in the American war on a small Asian country. "No Viet Cong," he says, "ever called me nigger."

The American military, desperate for public relations victories, introduces a new metric of success: the body count. The metric is meant to count up Viet Cong bodies, but as the American body count rises so do anti-war demonstrations in the streets. By November 1967, American troop strength in Vietnam approaches half a million in a conflict that eventually claims 15,058 Americans killed and 109,527 wounded. Violent clashes with police define the norm in defiant protests across the country. Draft cards burn in ritual bonfires, like bras a few years later. A former high school classmate goes underground after torching a university army recruiting center.

The seemingly endless turmoil escalates again in April 1967 when an anti-war march in New York City draws some three hundred thousand protestors. I am in Minneapolis in 1967, newly married, working through the hurdles to a PhD while sending anonymous anti-war satires to the *New York Review of Books*, which they ignore. I write to Robert Kennedy urging him to challenge President Johnson for the Democratic nomination, and I still have RFK's letter explaining why he won't oppose Johnson, a decision that he soon reverses.

Ten thousand protestors battle security forces outside the Chicago International Amphitheatre as the Democratic National Convention convenes in 1968, with TV cameras rolling. Prescient viewers might have noticed that Muhammad Ali is beginning to emerge as an outspoken pop culture sage, folk hero, and black icon, soon to achieve genuine global stature as an informal ambassador for Islam, peace, and racial justice. "I am America," he announces to a mostly unreceptive or uncomprehending audience of white American sports fans. "I am the part you won't recognize. But get used to me. Black, confident, cocky; my name, not yours; my religion, not yours; my goals, my own; get used to me."

"I was a soldier two weeks once in the beginning of the war, and was hunted like a rat the whole time": so recalls Samuel Clemens, better known as Mark Twain. Clemens, some fifteen years older than

THE GOOD SOLDIER

Newton, joins a Confederate militia in his native state of Missouri. Missouri enters the Union in 1820 as a slave state, under provisions of the Missouri Compromise, which simultaneously, tit for tat, admits Maine as a free state. Missouri is also the site of litigation resulting in the infamous 1857 Dred Scott decision by the Supreme Court, which held that slaves are not citizens and therefore slaves do not have the right to sue for freedom. Clemens, doubtless viewing such politico-legal chicanery with a skeptic's eye, serves with his militia unit for two weeks and sees live combat, until an overpowering Union force approaches. He and his fellow soldiers talk over their options—a democratic procedure—and decide to bolt. Freedom? An act of free choice? The military calls it *desertion*.

"Death-on-the-pale-horse-with-hell-following-after": this is how Clemens describes his brush with Civil War combat. The description suggests why Clemens responds much like his anti-hero Huck Finn, who ultimately rejects the world of civilized hypocrisies and lights out for the far west Indian Territory. Indian Territory has its own troubled relation with freedom. The U.S. government between 1830 and 1834 forcibly moves the Choctaw, Creek, Seminole, Cherokee, and Chickasaw tribes from southeastern states to land in present-day Oklahoma, set aside in 1834 and designated as Indian Territory. Clemens turns author only after the Civil War disrupts both his short-lived military career and his civilian employment as a Mississippi riverboat pilot. *Huckleberry Finn* appears in 1884, nearly twenty years after Lee's surrender, and it isn't an irrational stretch to read it as a sustained narrative meditation on the contradictory varieties of American freedom.

Huckleberry Finn, in a criminally truncated summary, describes the adventures of a runaway black slave and a runaway white boy who together make an improvised jailbreak for freedom. The action takes place in the 1830s and 1840s, when slavery is legal in Huck's home state of Missouri. Huck is running away from his abusive, drunken father, while Jim is running away from his owner, Miss Watson. Together they take to the open road, which in their case is the upper Mississippi River. Once on the river they are both free, apparently released from their different forms of bondage, albeit (there's the rub) temporarily. Freedom in America, especially for the unentitled and underprivileged, is almost always a transient, contingent, reversible condition. It is an "apparition," much as Emerson described nature, an *appearance*: the great American ghost-value that continuously vanishes before your eyes.

The freedom of the open road—mostly, the *apparent* freedom—constitutes a major theme in American fiction. From Whitman's *Leaves of Grass* (1855) and Jack Kerouac's *On the Road* (1957) to Ridley Scott's *Thelma and Louise* (1991), the open road as a path to freedom emerges as something like an American archetype, akin to the mythic rags-to-riches success story with which it regularly coincides. Benjamin Franklin, at the start of his own rags-to-riches story, describes escaping from the control of his older brother and—in another variant of the open road—leaving Boston by boat to become his own man. For Huck and Jim, unlike Franklin, the escape from confinement proves uncertain, incomplete, ambiguous, or impossible. Freedom, in American "road" fictions, is consistently misconstrued, more often lost than won. The biker played by actor-writer Dennis Hopper in the classic "road" film *Easy Rider* (1969) sums up in three words the freewheeling, countercultural, drugs-and-sex quest for freedom that he undertakes with a fellow biker named Captain America: "We blew it."

Huckleberry Finn invites an awareness that the river, like the open road and its freedom, constitutes a space of ambiguities. It is tenuously set apart, an ad hoc asylum where fathers, laws, and slaveholders no longer rule, but its apparent safety is also inherently unstable. The freedom that the river promises to Huck and Jim cannot last and cannot entirely insulate them from the surrounding land and its conflicts. Sociologist Hakim Bey calls such ambiguous spaces "temporary autonomous zones" (TAZ), as in the anarchic freedom of a pirate ship. Every TAZ, however, is always and only temporary. It survives as long as it takes authorities to reimpose social confinements and law. Huck's proposed solution—to light out for the Indian Territory—is an inherently unstable fantasy because the nation continues to gobble up land. When Huck and Jim begin their adventure in the early 1830s, there are twenty-one states. When *Huckleberry Finn* appears in 1884, the American flag has almost doubled its stars, to thirty-eight. The Indian Territory officially ceases to exist when Oklahoma in 1907 enters the Union as the forty-sixth state. One more temporary autonomous zone—one last fantasized escape route—is forever shut down.

OUT OF BONDAGE.

Huckleberry Finn concludes with a happy ending, of sorts, which it celebrates in the final illustration to the first edition with a curtain call that assembles Jim, Huck, and Tom Sawyer—with Jim's arms around the two young friends in appreciation and friendship (Figure 11). As if.

The caption "Out of Bondage" is double-voiced: simultaneously straight and skeptical. Twain chose the illustrator, and presumably he also approved the illustration and its caption. The three protagonists make an oddly mismatched trio, with Jim towering above Huck and Tom Sawyer, whose contrasting apparel reflects ways of being as different as head and heart. Is this really what freedom looks like? Or is freedom always imperfect, always compromised, always subject to new and perhaps less obvious forms of regulation?

CIVIL WAR *Duet*

There is something discordant beyond the size differential separating Jim and his two young white friends. The empty shackles that Huck holds up, as if for a congratulatory photo op, reflect both Jim's newfound freedom and its ambiguous status. Huck, that is, knows all along that Jim is free, just as Jim knows (after Pap's corpse floats past) that Huck is free: free without knowing it, in one sense of freedom. African Americans know very well that the exit from slavery ("out of bondage") is not the same as an entrance into freedom. Freedom for Jim—as for Huck and Tom in a different register—exists only within a public sphere where racism, religion, law, and government apply apparently inescapable constraints. The material handcuffs are only a prop in a melodramatic and unnecessary "rescue" staged by the ever-theatrical Tom Sawyer. The immaterial, mind-forged manacles that we wear within an imperfect, compromised political and cultural environment prove far harder, if not impossible, to recognize and escape.

Huck recognizes (even if he can't name them) some of the invisible shackles of civilized life that he longs to escape—but can't. The novel offers a semi-comic view of freedom as an American core value that Americans mostly fail to grasp or understand. It is a vision of freedom as always compromised, constrained, and—this is at least a thin straw of hope—still to-be-determined.

"Man is born free, and everywhere he is in chains," Rousseau writes famously in 1762, and his influential treatise does not refer to material shackles alone. It is during their initial escape to Jackson's Island—as Huck and Jim first break free from their different forms of confinement—that Huck comes to feel real affection for Jim. It is a dangerous, taboo affection—in radical conflict with religious proscriptions. Huck still struggles mightily with the counterclaims of church and friendship, but he ultimately arrives at a turning point where Twain's ironies and Huck's struggles both take a new direction. Huck's heart is "straightaway ethical" (to cite a concept from philosopher

Emmanuel Levinas). He *knows*, with an intuitive rightness, what to do. "All right, then," he decides, recognizing the bond that links him with Jim, "I'll go to hell."

Clemens' daughter, in a 1941 letter to the *New York Tribune*, recalls her father saying that the Civil War is "a blot on our history"—a history that includes the tragic spectacle of Americans killing Americans in a struggle over freedom—"but not as great a blot as the buying and selling of Negro souls."

Some twenty thousand Union soldiers and seventeen thousand Confederate soldiers are massing near the small Kentucky farming town of Perryville. Newton and Company D pitch camp somewhere among the growing multitude. Although Lewis Day thinks that his comrades dream of home, Newton may be dreaming of water. A drought has dried up springs and emptied ponds. Soldiers need water as much as they need bullets, beets, and letters from home. Thirst, as Day notes, often drives soldiers to drink water "wholly unfit for use." Such water, he adds, is "a fruitful source of disease." Moreover, the "horrid water" that soldiers drink constitutes "a never-ending source of trouble." Day has his facts straight about bad water. "It was the cause of many more deaths than all the Confederate lead that was fired."

Good, clean, fresh water proves so important that officers post armed guards around the few springs and small ponds still accessible—to keep order among the jostling soldiers and to run off the enemy. Newton sometimes walks miles in the evening to find water for cooking. As both armies converge near Perryville, Union forces under Major General Don Carlos Buell and Confederate forces under General Braxton Bragg are equally desperate for fresh drinking water.

In the early morning of October 8, 1862, Confederate forces launch what Lewis Day calls "a vigorous assault" to recapture the springs and ponds lost only a day earlier to Union troops. Thirst drives soldiers to take dangerous risks around the water holes. The inevitable skirmishes over water escalate into a full-scale military struggle. Suddenly, the Battle of Perryville is on.

Bloody fighting, sometimes hand-to-hand, rages on until darkness brings a temporary halt to the mass killing. Newton and Company D are receiving their awful initiation in battle, and now they know firsthand what Clemens meant when he called his brief experience in war "death-on-the-pale-horse-with-hell-following-after."

Historian Gary W. Gallagher in *The Union War* (2011) makes a case for what he calls a revisionist view, claiming that the dominant motive for the North is not opposition to slavery but preservation of the Union. Other historians challenge Gallagher's argument, which they say underestimates the significant religious and moral sentiment in the North opposing slavery, but this is not my call. The argument may be moot. Preservation of the Union soon becomes inseparable from military defeat of the Confederate states. The country, in any surviving postwar configuration, is simply incompatible with the system of enslavement. Newton does not write about slavery. Perhaps he feels that his personal opposition to slavery goes without saying, as needless to state directly, among family and fellow Ohio readers, as his opposition to evil.

Newton several times refers to the mission of his regiment as protecting and preserving *the old flag*. The Old Flag means the Union. He notes, without comment, that some old-flag protectors in

Company D hire former slaves (now legally documented freedmen) as servants and as cooks. The sight of black cooks mingling with the white officers and soldiers who hire them is by no means uncommon. Newton's only terse comment: *I cook my own provisions.*

The *Reflector* does not contain a dispatch describing the bloody events of October 8, 1862, at Perryville. Newton's gift for understatement now makes its masterpiece. No statement at all.

The Battle of Perryville, in one day, produces 8,848 men killed, wounded, or missing. Newton's silence might well express an encounter with the unspeakable. "For the time engaged," reports General Bragg, "it was one of the bloodiest and most hotly contested battles of the war." It is a battle with no clear winner: a minor tactical victory for Confederate forces, but a major strategic victory for the Union, which gains control of the crucial border state of Kentucky after Bragg inexplicably retreats to Tennessee. Neither commanding general, Bragg nor Buell, proves savvy. Civil War novelist and battlefield authority Jeff Shaara calls the Battle of Perryville "probably the best example in the entire war of utter incompetence on both sides."

How important is the Battle of Perryville? As Confederate General Basil Duke later reflects, "On the 10th of October more than fifty thousand Confederate soldiers were upon the soil of Kentucky." By the first of November, he continues, "they were all gone, and with them departed all hope, perhaps, of Southern Independence."

Newton acknowledges elsewhere that the dispatches he sends to the *Reflector* constitute *a general or formal* writing, unlike the informal letters home where *I can say what I pleas*e. While silent publicly, then, with no dispatch appearing in the *Reflector*, he writes a long letter home about the Perryville carnage in which he provides a personal account, factual and restrained, as if he feels in need of something more solid and stable than words to hang onto.

I did not see much of the battle-field of the late battle of Perryville or have firing. This plain introduction, as his letter proceeds, hardly tells the whole story, but nobody knows the whole story. Union General Buell, lacking information and located miles away from Perryville as late as noon, does not fully grasp the unfolding battlefield situation. He holds Company D in reserve until late afternoon, when random skirmishes stop and the full-scale regimental fighting begins. The gory ambiguous combat fought just west of Perryville turns the fertile rural farm country into an exploding obstacle course, as low-slung splitrail fences give cover to defenders and slow down attackers, with shells ripping the ground. Still at a distance, Newton hears both the cannon, sounding heavier than usual, and the sharp rattle of musket fire. Finally, in the afternoon, Company D receives orders to protect a Wisconsin artillery battery and moves from their wooded encampment toward an elevated position—less a well-defined hill than a continuous sloping mound—beside the Springfield Pike. Already the battle is looming closer and closer.

We came out from the wood and saw first one rebel wounded then one or two lying dead....

Newton and his fellow soldiers from Company D lie stomach-down in front of the Wisconsin battery as it keeps up a steady exchange of fire. Artillery plays a crucial role in supporting infantry brigades as they advance, as well as in knocking out opposing batteries. At Perryville, the battle lines shift as reserves are called in and units advance or fall back. Some Perryville units simply drop their arms and run. At any moment, a Confederate commander might send a squad on a flanking maneuver to take out the Wisconsin artillery. Newton on his stomach can't grasp what is happening as the smoke and booming sounds of battle roll past.

Perryville is a ghost town. Its four hundred residents have fled, but the hardest fighting occurs outside the town. Artillery units usually set up on high ground for the most effective shelling, but the elevation can leave them isolated and vulnerable. Hence the need for soldiers dug in to protect the batteries, as the enemy regards cannons as a valuable prize. Fire from Confederate artillery is already churning the ground near the Wisconsin position. A single cannon shell packs enough explosive to kill a dozen men. An incoming shell explodes fifteen feet in front of Newton. A few feet closer would have triggered an instant obituary in the *Reflector*. Luck matters, especially in battle.

Artillery batteries on the Union side consist of six twelve-hundred-pound bronze cannons, called *Napoleons*, each mounted on a mobile gun carriage carrying a supply of twelve-pound explosive shells. A team of six horses pulls the gun carriage on shoulder-high wheels. Panicked horses add to the chaos as the six Wisconsin cannons boom in sequence. Any horse hit by incoming fire turns a chaotic scene into surreal mayhem. A Confederate artilleryman describes the hellish scene when an incoming shell splinters their gun carriage. Terrified horses go "plunging and kicking, dashing out the brains of men tangled in the harness." Cannoneers with pistols crawl through the wreckage "shooting the struggling horses to save the lives of wounded men."

The hellish incoming artillery shells, as darkness falls, look to Newton *like balls of fire*. Lewis Day describes the crash of exploding shells, the smell and smoke of gunpowder, the yells of men rushing headlong at the enemy. "Go where the fire is hottest," Bragg orders Brigadier General St. John R. Liddell. ("The hottest place seemed to be everywhere," Liddell recalls.) The smoke-filled haze, darkening twilight, and the infamous fog of war all keep the Wisconsin artillerymen from knowing they are now within enemy lines. Or so Newton believes. The swelling hills and wooded ravines put visibility at near zero as the vague lines of battle shift.

Confederate General Leonidas Polk—famed as Sewanee's Fighting Bishop—can't tell whether the nearby troops firing at his soldiers are friend or foe. He rides ahead to reconnoiter. Suddenly, in the chaotic approaching darkness, he comes face-to-face with an entire Union regiment. Quick-witted, he takes advantage of the thunderous din, thick smoke, and twilight gloom—which help obscure his uniform and mask his voice—to impersonate a Union general. From his horseback elevation, he berates a nearby Union colonel and commands the soldiers to hold their fire. The guns obediently fall silent. Then, still impersonating a Union general, he slowly rides away. It doesn't take long before he returns to his troops and identifies the unknown shooters. "Every mother's son of them are Yankees!"

Polk's troops open fire. They instantly cut down two hundred men from the badly confused and silenced 22nd Indiana Regiment. God must be with the Bishop that night in Perryville.

Newton from his defensive position knows nothing about Polk's masquerade or the other massacres at the center of action where—in pockets and ravines, behind split-rail fences, across razed corn fields—the two vast armies clash. Bragg soon sees enough to understand that his seasoned Confederate veterans—while getting the better of Buell's green recruits—are badly outnumbered. As twilight deepens into darkness, he orders his battered troops to withdraw.

The final outcome of this terrifying, ambiguous long day's descent into blackness can't be fully assessed in military terms of victory or defeat. Numbers offer a better description. Worth repeating: 8,848 dead, wounded, or missing. The horror does not end when the shooting stops. Houses for miles around are pressed into service as makeshift surgeries. What Newton sees and hears in the midnight aftermath resembles the harrowing of hell: *the dead—the dying—those insane from their wounds & then piles of arms and legs that had been taken off.*

"We had never seen such a sight before," Lewis Day affirms. Dead and dying men are lying mixed together. "Others were awaiting their turn to be thrown upon the operating table, an old work-bench, while still others were being bandaged and patched up in various ways and assigned to this hospital or that...." Floorboards in Henry Bottom's bullet-raked farmhouse—once an ad hoc surgical theater—are still today stained dark with blood. Tooth marks indented into Minié balls show how soldiers coped during amputations. "The deep heartrending groans now and again heard, betokened suffering beyond expression," Day remembers. "Those of us who visited this terrible place came away sick at heart, but thankful that we had escaped unhurt."

Newton, sick at heart, is coming to understand what lies beneath his fantasies of military life. The 101st Ohio Regiment loses 219 men. ("We shall not all return.") Twenty percent of the force falls in a single indecisive battle. Confederate forces suffer even greater losses. Bragg's outnumbered army retreats under cover of darkness and marches the fifteen miles to Harrodsburg, where young women at Daughters College (an elegant Greek-revival mansion supposedly offering safety as well as education) have heard the cannons booming. Local churches take in some of the wounded, but by morning the battered army is on the move south to Tennessee. For three days, abandoned Confederate corpses lie unburied on the battlefield.

Henry Bottom runs a large farm just outside the town of Perryville, 760 acres, where much of the fighting raged. His farm is left "a wreck," as one soldier puts it: "it was all used up pretty much, everything." A stone fence is all that remains more or less intact. The explosive charge from an artillery shell sets fire to the barn, sparking an inferno that incinerates over one hundred wounded soldiers sheltering inside. It is Henry Bottom and several of his slaves who, after a few days of rising stench, collect the rotting corpses left on the battlefield and cover them in two massive pits. The deserted ground feels almost haunted as I walk through it one hundred and fifty years later. I'm not sure how anyone, Newton included, could endure bearing witness.

I saw a few of the dead and wounded. It was a hard sight—& I had no great desire to go over the field and see hundreds of dead and some of the dying who were not yet picked up. A cold rain sets in. Newton still has no tent—as he takes pains to mention in his letter home—but, soaked, cold, and sleepless, he imagines soldiers from both armies lying maimed and dying on the desolate, night-blackened farmland.

Oh what a night was Friday night to the poor wounded men who could not be stowed away in the hospital.

INTERLUDE
Postcolonial America

"The past is never dead. It's not even past."
—William Faulkner (1951)

America, once a collection of colonies governed by Great Britain, is not commonly regarded as a case study in postcolonialism. Postcolonial studies—as an academic discipline—tends to focus on Africa, India, South America, and the Middle East. The United States is usually classed among the major colonizing powers, seizing territory from Mexico and imposing colonial rule over Hawaii, Guam, and Puerto Rico: in short, acting like a traditional imperialist power carving out an overseas colonial domain. I want to flip the script. What if we think of America today not as an imperial power but as a postcolonial nation? What happens if we reimagine it as a land once colonized by European powers and still embodying the maladies of its postcolonial status? My question, while simple, entails a few related, preliminary queries.

Where does racism come from? Prejudice seems to be a fairly common human trait. But racism? How common is racism? My questions proliferate. Does racism, when it appears, depend on emotions, experiences, policies, ideas? I can't address these questions properly here, or even provide an accepted, consensus definition of racism. (We seem to be in the midst of a culture-wide process of redefinition.) Instead of seeking to define racism, I'd prefer to offer a brief and tentative descriptive account. Racism implies a belief in racial superiority. The racist believes that another race is not only inferior but also, to some degree, contemptible. Contempt implies an emotional charge that makes racism always more than a mere belief, but I would add one proviso. You can't have racism without the *idea* of race.

You can have snow—cold white fluffy stuff falling from the sky—without the *idea* of snow. If you fall asleep in the snow, hypothermia as a biological condition occurs without the *idea* of hypothermia. I would contend, however, that you can't have racism, whether as a social practice or as a personal belief, without the *idea* of race. The advantage of this pragmatic and belief-centered approach is that we pretty much know where the idea of race comes from.

The idea of race is not universal, ahistorical, or inevitable—and neither is racism. Both appear in human history at particular times and places. Most intellectual historians identify the idea of race as a product of the European Enlightenment. It emerges from the same era as such revolutionary, world-changing figures as Washington and Jefferson. The idea of race, however, requires more than a philosophical origin to explain the everyday practice of racism in America.

Racism in America, in addition to the idea of race, needs a perfect storm of three related historical phenomena: colonialism, the Atlantic slave trade, and the practice of chattel slavery. Chattel slavery—as distinct from other forms of enslavement—refers to a practice that classifies certain human beings as property to be bought, sold, or exchanged. Washington and Jefferson, as landowners, buy and sell slaves in normal, legal, commercial transactions. Slavery, of course, is not universally admired. Abolitionists, Evangelicals, and Quakers lodge early protests. In *Candide* (1759), Voltaire's dim-witted but ever-optimistic hero meets an African slave missing a hand and a leg. The slave explains that his master in Suriname (a South American colony owned by the Netherlands) punished him for attempting to run away. "This is the price," the slave patiently explains, as Voltaire weaponizes deadpan, "at which you eat sugar in Europe."

European colonialism and the Atlantic slave trade transform race from an abstract idea (embraced by distinguished Enlightenment rationalists) into emotionally charged, raw, callous, everyday, white-supremacist racism. Hume and Kant assert (as Jefferson too believes) that the Negro race is inherently inferior to whites, and this toxic idea ultimately provides a basis for the racism that allows European traders, bankers, and statesmen to engage in the ruthless production of slaved-based wealth, power, and empire. Racism not only provides Europe with sugar. It gives the colonial powers implicit permission to decimate native populations, to import more slaves, and to brutalize anyone who resists their enterprise. How so? Racism provides the convenient excuse that slaves and dark-skinned native people are inherently inferior to whites. Large-scale farmers such as Jefferson hire brutal overseers to punish slaves who prove disobedient or dangerous.

The sage of Monticello, who becomes the third president of the United States, fathers seven children with his slave-mistress, Sally Hemings. Jefferson also—as historian Jill Lepore shows in *These Truths* (2018)—takes the trouble to calculate, using algebraic symbols, the number of generations of interbreeding required to transform "pure negro blood" into the seven-eighths "portion of white" blood required by Virginia law to constitute *whiteness*. Slavery is a business—much like breeding horses—and racism oils the wheels of commerce. Voltaire's response to Jefferson, stripped of satire, might run like this: no matter how revolutionary your politics, no matter how much you personally dislike slavery, willful ignorance of the harm you cause is no excuse for turning a blind eye to your contributions to institutionalized racism. The brutality exercised upon slaves in the American South is clearly visible in photographs that reveal tangled masses of scars, like a grotesque flesh mat, or lynched black bodies hanging from trees.

Slave revolts in the New World colonies—some twenty-five organized revolts starting in the mid-sixteenth century—give Anglo-European colonial powers added incentive to justify racist attitudes toward African slaves. Militant slaves in the 1739 Stono Rebellion in South Carolina, for example, kill two dozen whites and burn six plantations. In response, the South Carolina legislature in 1740 enacts a ten-year moratorium on importing African slaves—as a means to develop (through genetic breeding) a more docile workforce of native-born blacks. They also start a school to teach Christian doctrine, presumably to indoctrinate slaves with such religious virtues as duty and submission that are directly beneficial to slaveholders. Reading and writing—skills considered dangerous for slaves to possess—have no place in the curriculum.

Here is my claim, offered with no pretense to originality. Enlightenment thinkers produce the idea of race at exactly the moment when colonial powers need an ideology of white superiority to justify ownership, exploitation, discipline, and punishment of African slaves. I don't claim that chattel slavery is the *sole* origin of twenty-first century racism, which no doubt absorbs multiple influences. Slavery, however, is a fundamentally new source of wealth that emerges between 1600 and 1800 when the Anglo-European and transatlantic slave trade combines with the mercantile expansion of colonial markets to crank up an unprecedented economic engine for the mass transfer of Africans to the New World. This mass transfer of people between continents for the purpose of selling them as slaves underwrites the new industrial economies of the West. It also goes hand-in-glove—this is my claim—with the invention of modern racism.

Slavery as a long-standing historical practice has no *necessary* relation to racism. In ancient times, Egyptians, Greeks, and Romans all keep household slaves, but minus racism. The Arab Islamic world enslaves Europeans, Africans, and fellow Arabs within an elaborate system of slave markets, but minus racism. Comanche raiders kidnap and enslave people from Native American tribes and pueblos, but minus racism. Certainly, the Catholic Church offers a religious justification for the brutality of Spanish conquistadors toward indigenous people, but white Europeans whom the Church regards as heretics face equally brutal torture and death. The commercial enterprise of buying and selling African slaves, as practiced during the period of Western colonial empire-building, is not only brutal and new but also largely responsible for making the invention of racism a philosophical, religious, and economic necessity. Racism and its premise of white supremacy prove exactly what god-fearing white slaveholders and slave traders need to carry out their self-interested roles in building a new world order.

The U.S. census for 1860 lists 3.95 million slaves, or 13 percent of the total population. How do 3.95 million Africans find their way to America? Who builds the ships? Who insures the fleets? Who profits from cargoes of black Africans? From London insurance brokers to Carolina planters, the web of interconnected economic interests helps explain the origins of racism in America. Once established on American soil, however, racism has proved so deeply entangled with a long and terrifying history of racial injustice as to prove impossible to root out.

The infamous triangular Atlantic slave trade produces the circulation of capital, goods, and human cargo that makes England, by the end of the eighteenth century, the supreme naval and economic powerhouse of Europe. "Rule, Britannia! rule the waves," as James Thomson's famous song directs. Set to music in 1740 at the height of the British overseas empire, the song follows its recurring imperative to "rule" with a line often forgotten in its ironies: "Britons never will be slaves." British liberty, defined loosely as freedom from tyrants, includes the practice of enslaving millions of Africans. Of course, in this commercial mass enslavement the British are following their Dutch, Portuguese, Spanish, and French competitors. A diagram suggests how elegantly this multicontinental economic slave-engine functioned (Figure 12).

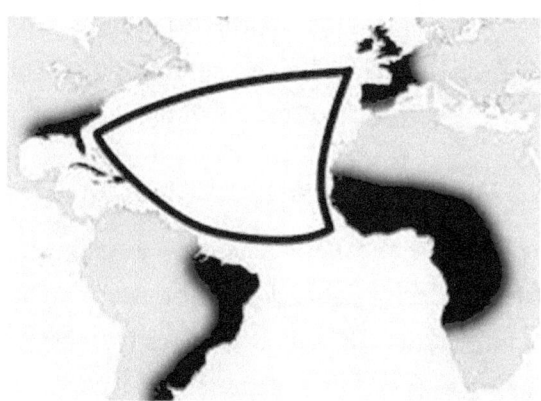

A ship leaves Liverpool, say, loaded with products manufactured in England's new industrial factories that poet-prophet William Blake describes as "dark Satanic mills." In Africa, the ship trades those industrial goods (guns, ironware, glass, textiles) for slaves, pocketing in the exchange a handsome profit. Next, the slave ship transports its human product to the West Indies, to South America, and to the American colonies, where the owners pocket another handsome profit as, in exchange, they take on raw materials such as sugar, tobacco, and cotton for the return to England.

The problem with diagrams is that they do not account for human suffering. A diagram or even a photograph can't adequately indicate the horrors that unfold on the five-thousand-mile Middle Passage across the Atlantic, when captive blacks are chained in cargo holds so oxygen-poor that candles gutter out. Thousands die during the voyage—their bodies tossed overboard. The term *cargo*, from a Spanish verb meaning "to load," dates from the time of the commercial slave trade, and its application to captives—reducing humans to the status of lumber or dry goods—sums up the dehumanization that slavery entails, as contemporary advertisements make clear (Figure 13).

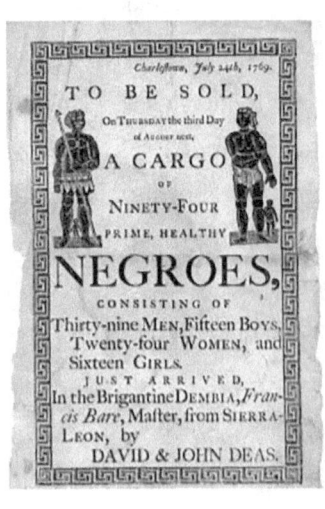

The Atlantic slave trade is an all-white, racist, money-making machine that traffics in black bodies.

All you need in order to conduct this unpleasant business with a clear conscience is a racist ideology that regards blacks as inferior to whites—and as less than fully human. Presto. Ideologies work well because people captured within their spell do not generally recognize that they are spellbound. They don't see themselves as shaped by a dominating idea that also shapes how they see the world, much as Americans today are shaped and see the world within the context of a capitalist ideology. "Look out kid / they keep it all hid," sings Bob Dylan in "Subterranean Homesick Blues" (1965): "Twenty years of schooling and they put you on the day shift." Dylan's line suggests a deliberate adult conspiracy—adults against kids, them against us—but ideology keeps adults as well as kids constrained, as if by the unseen force of gravity.

The slave trade in the early capitalist West seems as inevitable as the California gold rush or Henry Ford's production line. Dylan, after all, depends on Columbia Records to release his song as a single—his first Top 40 hit—and then as the lead track on his album *Bringing It All Back Home*. How many young adults like me sign up for a monthly mail order subscription to the Columbia Record Club? (Our dorm rooms soon overflow with unwanted album selections that students forget to decline.) Capitalism as an ideology—in its all-absorbing power—can absorb even Dylan's protests against capitalism.

In 1781, with a mysterious disease killing both African captives and crew, Captain Luke Collingwood of the British slave ship *Zong* orders 130 Africans thrown overboard, alive. On his return to England, he files an insurance claim to cover the financial loss. Insurance is an unseen hand indispensable to the capitalist slave trade. Edward Lloyd starts his informal coffee-house brokerage in 1680s London—a meeting place for ship owners and underwriters—which today, as Lloyd's of London, provides the world-famous mutualized marketplace where syndicates and underwriters share the financial risks involved in the latest big capitalist ventures.

Americans today don't think of themselves as a colonized people. The Fourth of July is about fireworks and hot dogs—not the overthrow of a colonial oppressor—but we are nonetheless a postcolonial nation. The legacy of the slave trade keeps the poison of colonial racism locked in our bones.

I am putting in play here ideas about underlying historical currents, and I know that an interlude cannot do them justice. The greater injustice is to ignore them. Such currents constitute the invisible environment that envelops Newton as the artillery shells explode around him at Perryville. They are conceptual realities as material, stolid, and well defended as Fort Mitchel. Newton is not beyond the reach of ideologies. Nor are we. We see the world within ideologies that shape how we see Native Americans, Jews, Italians, Asians, Latinos, women, gays, transgender people, children, and the poor. African Americans living in disadvantaged neighborhoods know that freedom and equality as an everyday experience still await the transition from flag-waving rhetoric into good schools, clean water, and safe streets.

Does the 101st Ohio Infantry include black soldiers? Probably not. The Union Army includes 178,975 African American soldiers, and the overall percentage of black soldiers runs at about 6.7 percent. An average regiment of 1,000 soldiers, then, would in theory include about 67 free blacks, but there is no average regiment. The U.S. military maintains an official policy that keeps black soldiers in units separate from whites. (The policy remains in place until 1948.) Black soldiers serve in all-black units. In May 1863 Congress establishes the U.S. Bureau of Colored Troops for the purpose of managing black enlistees, but the policy doesn't go smoothly. In *Ohio's Black Soldiers Who Served in the Civil War* (2014), Eric Eugene Johnson explains that Ohio starts late in raising its first all-black regiment, the 127th Ohio Volunteer Infantry. Ohio governor David Tod (in office during 1863) believes that blacks should not be allowed to serve as soldiers. Johnson acknowledges that his account may overlook many black soldiers from Ohio—"particularly those who served in Ohio's white volunteer regiments." I have found no one who can say with certainty whether any African American soldiers served with Newton in the 101st Ohio Volunteer Regiment.

A number of blacks who are not soldiers *accompany* the 101st Infantry—as cooks or personal servants. "We find a good many negroes here who are ready to go along with us," writes Colonel Stem, back when the 101st begins its march into Kentucky. He disapproves of these roadside transactions. He knows that some blacks are escaped slaves and invite confrontations with bounty hunters and slaveholders. "I have not witnessed any of these performances, don't know that they are so and don't want to know anything about it," Stem admits to his wife: "I should not allow the men to coax darkies away nor shall I aid in restoring them to their master unless ordered to do so by my superiors."

Colonel Stem uses *darkey* as interchangeable with *negro*, but, despite its link with plantation life in the South, he does not use the term as a racial slur. In *Forbidden American English* (1990), Richard Spears contends that *darkey* was once considered polite usage. Stephen Foster's "My Old Kentucky Home" (1853)—adopted in 1928 as the state song of Kentucky—originally contained the line "'Tis summer, the darkies are gay." No longer polite usage in 1986, "darkies" is replaced by the innocuous term "people." Foster, a northerner by birth, meant his song to encourage a respect for blacks notably absent from minstrel shows, but Newton may pay his respects by avoiding the term *darkey* altogether. He refers once, in correct military usage, to a *colored* regiment, but more is at stake than correct usage. Racism in America is inseparable from words that perpetuate it, often hurled like insults with the intent to offend, incite, and injure.

"The negroes of the Reg't are in the habit of marching in the rear of the Reg't...." So writes another officer in the 101st, Lt. Isaac Rule of Company I. He most likely is referring to cooks and servants. Or are there also a few free black soldiers marching at the back of the column? Doubtful, but I don't know. Union armies include a total of 5,092 black soldiers from Ohio. Frederick Douglass encourages free black men to volunteer for the Union army as a way to ensure eventual full citizenship. Even all-black Union regiments, however, are led by white officers.

Captain Jay C. Butler of Company B—while lamenting his loss of "one of the best negroes"—provides an insight into how white soldiers regard their black servants: "He could cook, wash, carry a knapsack, dance, laugh and sing." "We had congratulated ourselves upon our good success," he adds, defining success in a white-only metric, pleased at finding such a multi-talented servant, but then the tale turns dark. The man's "master" appears and claims his runaway slave while the 101st is marching through Kentucky. Butler, whose comments focus on his personal loss of a useful servant, indirectly acknowledges the vicious, inevitable punishment that follows the capture and return of a runaway: "He was about scared to death...."

"He was a great help to us," Butler remarks. "I could get along very well while he carried my knapsack."

Newton carries his own knapsack. He also calls upon his religious education in which all people—the poor in fact holding a spiritual advantage over the rich—are equal before God. The first president of Oberlin College, Asa Mahan, is a noted social reformer and abolitionist. Founded by missionaries, Oberlin is the first American college to admit black students. George Vashon in 1844 is the first black student at Oberlin to earn a bachelor's degree. Mary Jane Patterson, in 1862, is the first black woman to earn a degree from any American college. The town of Oberlin is also a key stop along the Underground Railroad, with its network of safe houses helping runaway slaves on their backroad journey to freedom. Newton's religious upbringing, his Oberlin College education, and Oberlin's reputation for abolitionist sentiment give him good reason to see the war as more than a conflict over states' rights or a defense of the old flag.

Christmas Eve 1862 brings an unexpected gift for soldiers of the 101st Infantry: "bright new Springfield rifles."

The new Springfield rifles, as Lewis Day reports, replace the heavy Lorenz firearms that he calls "Austrian horrors." Springfield rifles, in fact, become the most common weapon used during the war. Lighter, more reliable, and more accurate than Austrian muskets, the Springfield rifles can hit a target at five hundred yards and fire three shots per minute. "We went wild over the change and acted much like little boys with new sleds," Day continues. "At once we became anxious to try our new guns on the enemy—nor had we long to wait."

It is not all eagerness, however, not after Perryville. What does Newton think about the new rifles? He doesn't say. *I stood picket guard about 2 hours in a hard rain the other night.*

What is it like to stand for hours in the woods, pitch dark, in a cold rain, then sleeping with no tent, covered only with an oilcloth blanket as the approaching winter temperature drops? Sheer survival no doubt weighs heavier than reflections on slavery, race, or new rifles. This is not magical realism. It is an eighteen-year-old soldier from Ohio sleeping in the mud and cold. His immediate prospect is more combat, more corpses, and more terror. He does not choose Samuel Clemens' hasty exit.

Christmas, then, does not look particularly merry and bright. An unreasonably optimistic temperament, which I share with Newton, may be more useful to him now than any weapon. But I am looking ahead. Newton has not quite yet arrived at Christmas Eve. After the late-October trauma of Perryville, he must first endure a long and dismal November, perhaps, in his more reflective moments, passing through something like what Ishmael in *Moby Dick* (1851), just a few years earlier, calls "a damp, drizzly November in my soul."

PART TWO
Life on the Road

"The Way is not difficult,
just avoid picking and choosing."
—Seng-Ts'an (d. 606)

NOVEMBER 1862: NASHVILLE

I sometimes feel as if I were way out ... separated from all the world where no friend could hear me but God!

Newton never mentions a companion, not even Beman. He confides these desolate feelings in a letter home, four months after he mustered in. He has survived the slaughter at Perryville, and the ritual patriotism of rallying around the old flag has begun to wear thin. Military life doesn't fit comfortably with the values of an earnest young man raised in a religious home, whose thoughts include postwar preparations for the ministry. Oberlin College maintains the religious outlook of its co-founding Presbyterian clerics, who emphasize the Christian virtues and moral principles that they find lacking—to put it mildly—among American settlers in the West. Newton now spends his days, as he writes home, almost constantly *in the midst of influences that tend to debase one's mind.*

Loneliness seems inescapable. Newton takes no pleasure and no part in what he calls *the vulgar jokes of camp life*. At Hamilton College, I too feel out of place, not friendless, but not knowing where my place is. Hamilton, then an all-men's college, occupies a rural hilltop where marooned young males disparage everyone outside their immediate social circle as "assholes." Easy stuff, compared to what Newton feels, but I can imagine even worse loneliness. Suppose there is no God to hear him. Suppose that God is simply the Supreme Fiction. Luckily, Newton cannot entertain such thoughts. Religious faith and moral values give his life a firm grounding, despite moments when he feels cut off and isolated. For his sake, I'm glad he does not share my doubts.

The average Civil War soldier is twenty-six years old. Newton at eighteen joins a distinctly older group. He forages nightly for food and water, cooks his own meals, and stands picket duty with fellow soldiers who know nothing about the Greek and Latin classics that still constitute the groundwork for a ministerial life. For now, Newton is one sparrow among a multitude of armed sparrows that he believes God numbers and watches over amid this brutal conflict. A native optimism can help him through friendlessness, fear, and hardship, but it is no match for feelings of despair. The feeling of separation that he experiences, as confided in his November letter, does not resemble the peace and transcendence of Romantic solitude but something more like anguish. Faith does not guarantee that God will hear or answer his prayers. It is to his mother that Newton addresses his most heartfelt request: *O pray for me that the Holy Spirit may lead my mind out to high and true thoughts so that I shall grow not earthward but heavenward.*

News on the military front remains bad. In April 1862, some four months before Newton musters in, Ohio loses two thousand soldiers in the disastrous Battle of Shiloh. Six months later, the Battle of Perryville in October is at best a bloody stalemate, with corpses everywhere. On November 4, Company D breaks camp in Kentucky and crosses into Tennessee for what promises to be hard fighting ahead, in pursuit of Bragg's retreating army. Significant noncombat casualties, however, are now beginning to mount. Lewis Day notes the erosion of regimental strength. "The 101st left sixty boys sick in the hospital ... when we began our march to the South."

I had a bad night last night, Newton writes on November 9. *I have quite a hard cough*. Newton's usual assurances that he is well—which he knows his family wants to hear, despite assurances that he'll write the *unvarnished truth*—carry a barely concealed shift in emphasis. His health continues to occupy his letters as more than a passing topic. One week later his cough has improved, but the steady concern with his physical state introduces a new note. *I am well, entirely well*, he writes home on November 16, perhaps protesting a bit too much. *Entirely* well is not the entire story, or maybe the entire story now includes a few well-chosen, mildly dissonant notes easy to ignore in a trailing clause. *My health was never better only that I have a slight cold.*

A slight cold and even a hard cough are understandable complaints, given the changing late-autumn weather and a soldier's life outdoors. Newton, after Perryville, nonetheless seems far more attentive to health and illness. Diarrhea, hardly a topic for letters home, now makes its appearance as an unavoidable byproduct of an everyday diet in which hardtack and coffee provide the staples, along with occasional salt pork, corn meal, and whatever else soldiers can scavenge on the march. Foraged roots and fetid water are sometimes all Newton has to work with in preparing dinner. Unwelcome anytime, diarrhea is the predictable companion of such a diet, and it quickly turns downright dangerous—even lethal—when combined with dehydration.

Health is starting to become a significant issue for Company D. Soldiers aren't on the lookout for pathogens in the days before germ theory, but sickness can prove as insidious as bushwhackers. Michael Sherer of Company E falls sick with typhoid fever and dies in camp, buried under the branches of a young cedar "in great solemnity," according to Lewis Day. Company D loses William Merritt to illness. "He never was very strong since he enlisted," Beman Read tells the *Reflector*. Long marches, cold nights, bad diet, and diarrhea—together with picket duty and hard rain—are taking a toll. Company D starts out from Camp Monroeville one hundred men strong. The unit looks very different when Newton writes on November 20.

At times we have had so many back on the road sick or present & unfit for service that we could not muster more than 40 fit for duty.

Duty is a key value in Newton's moral outlook, but the body is lodging its claims. Mortality is in the air. Many soldiers give their cash to the chaplain with instructions about who should receive it if (or, as appears more likely every day, when) they die. The open road, for weary, sick, and simply unfit soldiers in the Civil War, does not unfold in Whitmanesque democratic vistas of glowing health but increasingly serves to mark the grave sites of fallen comrades. Illness knows no rank. A few days before the death of private Merritt, Captain W. C. Parsons of Company E is taken sick during a long march and dies. Newton, while proud about doing his duty as a soldier, increasingly in his letters home seems to notice the costs of duty, in lost health and wasted lives.

Bad news on the military front beginning to filter back home via newspaper reports may help explain why Newton fills his letters home with reassurances. His health seems to be as changeable as the weather. In late November, he notes that he is *growing fat*. Maybe there is even a gain in well-being from surviving his rugged outdoor life. Despite some setbacks, hard nights, and diarrhea, his physical condition seems generally improved, and the dark friendless shadow of anguish and despair appears to have passed by. Appearances are mostly all that a soldier can rely on, and they are almost always unreliable. A letter home in late November concludes with an extremely upbeat, unreliable report. *I don't think I ever had better health than at present.*

I am astonished. Delaware in 1865 votes *against* ratifying the Thirteenth Amendment. Delaware finally recants a generation later ... in 1901. Bad news, but there is worse. Kentucky, Lincoln's birthplace, doesn't approve the Thirteenth Amendment until ... 1976. Mississippi (unbelievably) waits until 2013! It's no surprise that racism is so hard to root out when state legislatures can't manage to agree, with the Constitution, that neither slavery nor involuntary servitude shall exist in the United States. Racism is impossible to outlaw even if slavery has been defeated, and nothing but racism can account for the foot-dragging process of ratification. Such episodes feed a new respect I feel for individuals, early on, who not only know that slavery is wrong but also work hard to oppose it, often at great personal risk. I'm referring specifically to the loose alliance of outspoken nineteenth-century anti-slavery activists and reformers known as abolitionists.

Abolitionists for me have mostly meant John Brown, the grim, fiery prophet of race war, who with his followers hacks to death five pro-slavery men in Bleeding Kansas. Daguerreotypes show a forbidding figure who appears gripped by a personal mission, or seized by inner demons, unyielding, with a wide straight mouth that cuts across his face like a surgical incision (Figure 14).

Zealots, even in a good cause, make me uneasy, and John Brown is an abolitionist super-zealot. His direct line to God persuades him that a violent slave uprising—nothing short of an all-out race war—is the only means for ending slavery. He becomes a martyr among northern admirers after he is captured and executed for his failed raid on the federal arsenal at Harper's Ferry, Virginia, seeking to secure weapons for his slave revolt. Abolitionists, however, as I'm learning, do not necessarily pledge allegiance to John Brown. They include a diverse alliance of writers, preachers, activists, religious societies, women's groups, and academics, with Quakers among the earliest opponents of slavery. They cannot be lumped together as stiff, self-righteous, strait-laced, sanctimonious, third-generation puritans. Harriet Tubman alone, an escaped slave who during the Civil War serves as an army spy and scout, contradicts my caricature of abolitionists. Some may possess more than a dash of John Brown craziness, but the mostly white, activist, committed northerners also choose to put their lives in danger on behalf of blacks.

William Lloyd Garrison ranks among the most important anti-slavery activists. His religious and moral principles turn him resolutely against the practice of slavery well before Newton is born or the nation splinters into civil war. His attitude toward slavery is simple and straightforward: he detests it. His mild, almost scholarly demeanor, right down to the trademark spectacles, seems in sync with his long-standing pacifist beliefs, but the set jaw and intense gaze reflect his unyielding and uncompromising opposition to a treatment of blacks that he regards as downright evil (Figure 15).

His speeches and writing often evoke reason as the most appropriate, God-given instrument for opposing slavery, but he is hardly an embodiment of calm rationality. He is impassioned in nonviolence, and the eradication of slavery grips him, as it does John Brown, like a mission sent by God. Tactics matter, however, and a bloody race war is exactly what Garrison wants to avoid. For thirty-five years he keeps up relentless public pressure against slaveholders and slavery, especially in the weekly newspaper that he co-founds in 1831, *The Liberator*. He writes most of the articles, sets the type, and almost single-handedly publishes the leading anti-slavery journal of his day—and it was a very long day—from January 1, 1831 until December 29, 1865.

His courageous public opposition to slavery proves so effective that Georgia offers a large bounty for his capture. A mob once drags him from his Boston office, and only a last-minute police rescue saves him.

Reason—or so Enlightenment thinkers such as Garrison believe—is the internal voice of God. While John Brown hears the vengeful God of the Old Testament, Garrison hears the loving, merciful, reasonable

God of the New Testament. With Scripture as his guide, Garrison provides the abolitionist cause with a peace-loving, nonviolent, and reason-based alternative to firebrand tactics and insurrection. He has reason to believe that his approach will be effective because a few slaveholders do indeed change their ways, often on religious grounds. Long before the Civil War, Robert Carter, a prominent Baptist plantation owner in Virginia, gains fame (or, in some quarters, infamy) for freeing his five hundred slaves. Although 90 percent of blacks in Delaware are free by 1860, freedom for blacks in border states such as Delaware cannot serve as a reliable basis for protection. Vigilantes treat renegade white slave holders in the Old South who dare to free their slaves much as they treat captured runaways. Carter was lucky. Others are summarily lynched.

Garrison publishes the first issue of *The Liberator* in his mid-twenties and leaves no doubt that its young author, while opposed to violence, does not confuse rationality with self-restraint. Slavery calls for an excessive and passionate speech that he wields like a broadsword:

> On this subject, I do not wish to think, or speak, or write, with moderation. No! no! Tell a man whose house is on fire, to give a moderate alarm; tell him to moderately rescue his wife from the hands of the ravisher; tell the mother to gradually extricate her babe from the fire into which it has fallen; – but urge me not to use moderation in a cause like the present. **I am in earnest— I will not equivocate— I will not excuse— I will not retreat a single inch— AND I WILL BE HEARD.**

Heard he is. Lincoln later credits abolitionists with altering his own views on slavery. The credit is more than a rhetorical gesture. At the war's end, Lincoln invites Garrison—now sixty and worn out from four decades of tireless struggle—to raise the Union flag in a ceremony held, significantly, where the war began: at the recaptured Fort Sumter.

CIVIL WAR *Duet*

Camp rumors say that Lincoln has replaced McClellan with Burnside. Is it true? Yes. Did General Jefferson Davis—a disconcerting name for a Union commander—really shoot fellow Union general "Bull" Nelson? Yes again. Rumor sometimes travels slowly. It was back in September 29, 1862, when, after a quarrel and insults, the diminutive Davis—no relation to the president of the Confederacy—returns with a loaded pistol and kills William "Bull" Nelson. Many soldiers feel that Nelson, a large and notorious bully, got what he deserved. Then comes mail call. So it goes in Beman Read's chatty report to the *Reflector*. Yes, the 101st appears to be following the route of Bragg's army as it retreats into Tennessee. "Our camp ground is a good one, but we have to go quite a distance for water," Beman writes, "which is not very pleasant." Is Beman taking over Newton's role as correspondent?

Beman might have noted that the weather is unusually dry for early November as the newly battle-tested soldiers, in the dreadful aftermath of Perryville, march, wait, drill, forage, and stand yet more picket duty. This daily regimen may provide the surrogate workouts that prompt Newton to say he's never felt in better health.

It is the mid-1970s, and I am on leave from the University of Iowa. The William Andrews Clark Memorial Library—my destination—occupies a walled, city-block compound hidden within the black section of Los Angeles that I remember as home to the 1965 Watts riots: five days of race-based fire and fury. The library, in a two-story Italianate villa constructed to house Clark's extensive book collection, specializes in eighteenth-century British literature. It now belongs to UCLA, and as a card-carrying scholar of eighteenth-century British literature I feel entitled to send a last-minute request for a residency while I pursue a yearlong research project for which I've received a Guggenheim Fellowship. I am mildly surprised when The Clark—as its band of devotees call it—grants my request and offers me the use of a carrel.

My residency extends to the fall semester only, but I am eager to leave Iowa City after my marriage with Dee breaks up, and one semester at least justifies the long Jeep ride west. I feel immediate regret once I see the location of my carrel, in a windowless basement. Who doesn't fear earthquakes? Will archaeologists excavate me a few centuries after The Big One brings Los Angeles to its knees? Angelenos—a breed apart—proceed as if the inevitable megaton earthquake predicted by psychics and seismologists alike won't happen on their watch. I imagine future scholars trying to make sense of a thirty-year-old male skeleton buried, Pompeii-like, under mounds of literary rubble associated with—how odd!—eighteenth-century England.

Bill Clark, unaccountably, did not equip his library with a gym. Its few carrels are a tightly guarded prize, so I count myself lucky to have a place to work, but work constitutes only one leg of my life-triangle. Love, Work, and Fitness. I depend on all three, but love is now MIA, and work isn't going all that well. Fitness thus takes on exaggerated import in filling up the emptiness in my one-legged lapsed triangle. Newton and I seem to share a concern for bodily health, although he gives no evidence of gym-style vanity and faces live ammunition. In any case, I arrive each morning an hour before The Clark opens its doors and, in the interim, run laps around the shaded, parklike landscape. There is only one problem. The LA heat. As The Clark's officious director personally opens the doors, I greet him each morning in a sweat-stained shirt with my hair dripping wet. He appears to find this self-presentation, as even I can sense, unpleasing. Clearly, I fail to meet his standards of scholarly decorum. I'm not surprised to receive a letter informing me that The Clark declines to renew my residency for the spring semester.

I have no regrets, as research and the Clark Library have suddenly lost their appeal. On my excursion to LA, through a sequence of highly improbable events, I have just fallen in love with Ruth. Springtime belongs to lovers, books can wait for fall, and Ruth soon changes my life.

I miss sabbaths.
Newton's letters home speak from the heart. His plain statement about missing the Sabbath—always set apart at home for worship—perfectly reflects the gap that separates him from many of his fellow soldiers, but not all. Regiments travel with chaplains, and Civil War photos show chaplains conducting religious services for throngs of soldiers. For Company D, Sundays on the road are also set aside for inspections—which means that soldiers devote much time early on Sunday to *preparing* for inspection. Newton writes that sometimes he can't find even a brief interval to open his Bible.

He usually addresses his most intimate thoughts about matters religious and spiritual, including his disappointments, directly to his mother: *You know that there is a kind of sabbath atmosphere that we breathe in,—but that is not so here in camp.*

Newton apparently comes to accept the loss of a spiritual atmosphere on the Sabbath, as he mentions it only once. He has urgent material issues to address. In a letter home as the fall days edge toward chilly, drizzly late November, he asks his family to send him ... *mittens.*

LIFE ON THE ROAD

*R*uth loved to tell the story of how we met. Her scholarly father, Ralph Cohen, whom I knew from my first teaching job at the University of Virginia, invites me to a party in Los Angeles at the home of an academic friend. Ralph's colleagues describe him as "rabbinical," which I construe as shorthand for any Jewish intellectual devoted to close textual analysis. I don't hold high romantic expectations when told that the party will likely include Ralph's daughter, Ruth. My dissertation director and (later) friend, Sam Monk, has asked Ralph to look after me in LA, and at the party Ralph enlists his wife to help him introduce me to eminent UCLA scholars. We do not yet use the word "networking," which is what Team Cohen undertakes on my behalf, but, as with the director of the Clark Library, I turn out to be a serious disappointment. No matter how diligently the Cohens introduce me to bigwigs well situated to advance my academic standing, whenever they check I am back on the sofa talking with Ruth.

Ruth is an exotic beauty, with brown eyes, long black hair, and a dancer's body. I have never met anyone like her. We talk and talk. Later that evening she calls the tennis pro she is dating and breaks up over the phone. "No discussion?" he asks, taken aback. "No," says Ruth.

Ruth ultimately joins me in Iowa City, quitting her job as head of technical services at the USC Norris Medical Library. Am I leaving out all the juicy parts? Of course. It isn't a silk-smooth transition, there are bumps in the road, and we have lots of mutual learning ahead. Ruth retains vestiges of what I call her LA "glaze." Although she is two years younger than me, the glaze makes young women look older and older women look younger, which may be its purpose in ageless LA. It doesn't play as well in Iowa. I tease Ruth about her long, painted fingernails. How can she manage the demands of a vegetable garden? Yes, we both have much to learn, stereotypes to get past, but we manage, lovingly. Ruth's intensity, reflected unmistakably in an ominous tightening of her lips, has the power to cut through my non-confrontational style.

Once, frustrated at the pettiness of academic life, I make a dismissive comment about an academic article I'm working on. "I never want to hear you talk like that again," Ruth says fiercely—her lips tightening—and I never do.

I never yet have had a feeling of regret at the course I have chosen.

This is a remarkable statement unless Newton is completely self-deceived. It comes after his first taste of battle—horrific—and after his despairing confession of feeling friendless and isolated. He not only reaffirms his choice to enlist but also seems able to forget, deny, or overcome his own doubts. A temperamental stubbornness, which I share, may serve him well in surviving hard times. I prefer to think of my stubbornness as persistence. Persistence is at least a minor virtue, a mode of standing firm in the face of obstacles, no matter what. Newton stands firm in his choice. Duty—including the duty of Sunday inspections—is persistence turned inside out: you accept, willingly, an obligation imposed as if from an outside power.

Duty first, then. But pleasure? Is there space in Newton's world for frivolity or cutting loose? Beman Read, free from chaplain services and inspection, one Sunday sets out alone, curious to see a nearby town recently occupied by Rebel forces. He is surprised to find the town almost deserted. He stops at one still-occupied house, where a woman invites him in for dinner. Maybe loneliness, courtesy, or his military uniform prompts the invitation, but, regardless, a temporary truce seems acceptable to both parties. "The lady said she had strong

Southern principles," Beman reports, "but we had no difficulty on that account, for I wanted the dinner."

Hunger appeased, Beman walks back to camp where Newton, also free from the regular Sunday inspection, is no doubt pursuing his own private and personal Sabbath meditations.

Two days later Newton and Beman are both on the march again—still looking for drinkable water—headed toward Nashville and toward what Lewis Day reports as an almost certain battle. Reliable information, however, is as scarce as clean water. Newton is now a veteran of temporary camps and countless marches. The nights are growing colder. Have the mittens arrived? His prevailing mindset seems a combination of not-knowing, persistence, and just making do.

How long we shall stay here, or where we shall go, I have not the least idea —We have no tents, but sleep on the ground with our oil cloth blankets over us.

The woman who precedes me at the podium in New York City, where I am about to receive a 1992 PEN award for *The Culture of Pain*, has written a prize-winning memoir about her dysfunctional family. I improvise an opening remark about how grateful I am for my family, one hundred percent functional, and I look directly into the audience at my parents, Emily and Tony. They have driven from Wilmington for the presentation. Somehow, on the modest income of a family physician, they raise five independent and (so far as I know) drug-free children, putting them through college debt-free. We are a close-knit group despite our staggered ages and diverse temperaments, a diversity that our parents seem to like and to nurture. Our severest blow as a family is the death of Elizabeth. Elizabeth, only sister to four lucky brothers, is a beautiful, vibrant redhead just coming into her own powers as campus minister at the University of Maine.

It is 1993, and Elizabeth has just turned forty. As she is driving home with her nephew Jason from a poetry reading by Allen Ginsberg, a large cement chunk hurtles down from an overpass and instantly kills her. Is it an accident? Did bored kids or troublemakers throw the chunk down? Maine's notorious potholes and the state's crumbling infrastructure might be to blame. The police have no leads. As the eldest son, it falls to me to contact my parents. When I call, they have just walked in the front door, returning from an extended trip to Spain. My father answers the phone, and I speak the unspeakable words that Elizabeth is dead. He repeats my words aloud, as if struggling to understand. "*Our* Elizabeth?" I will never forget my mother's wild scream in the background.

Her four brothers process our grief in different ways. I contact a noted landscape architect at the University of Maine and commission the design for a memorial garden at the Wilson Center: Elizabeth's professional home as campus minister. Compassionate, loving, spiritual, and undeterred by her own struggles, which include coming out as gay, she was a lifelong activist devoted to peace and social justice. She introduced me to liberation theology and—always willing to nudge us gently beyond our comfort zones—introduced family members, young and old, traditional and progressive, to anatomically correct dolls for children.

Elizabeth came closest to living a life of the spirit that resembles the devoted ministerial life of (not quite yet) ex-soldier Newton Brown.

"When Johnny Comes Marching Home," the popular song published in 1863, does not mention tents, rain, or diarrhea.

LIFE ON THE ROAD

Johnny's sanitized homecoming is also deferred to some future-perfect time. The immigrant Irish American bandleader Patrick Gilmore supposedly composes the song for his sister, anxiously awaiting the return of her artillery captain fiancé. Gilmore will not disturb her with realism.

> The village lads and lassies say
> With roses they will strew the way
> And we'll all feel gay
> When Johnny comes marching home.

Village lads and lassies tossing rose petals? The pure Irish blarney seems well suited to the singsong, childlike, monosyllable rhymes. It is stirring music, to be sure: sentimental, catchy, and joyously simplistic. No injuries, no trauma, no regrets.

Emily Dickinson in Massachusetts has other thoughts as she watches military homecomings, no doubt half-hidden behind the Amherst curtains. She recognizes the power of spectacle and the desire to claim victory, but she also acknowledges the unwelcome truth that Civil War homecomings often involve crutches and caskets. Any present elation—unlike the fantasy future when "we'll all feel gay"—proves so fleeting as to undermine altogether the concept of triumph. When the drums stop, their silence exposes wartime military celebrations as little more than noise and illusion.

> My Triumph lasted till the Drums
> Had left the Dead alone
> And then I dropped my Victory.

The abandoned dead, alone after all the drumming and fine speeches, remain as witness to the hollowness of public honor—and perhaps the futility of war. "It dropped so low in my regard," as Dickinson writes in another poetic image of homespun disillusion, "I heard it hit the ground."

CIVIL WAR *Duet*

The Civil War not only accounts for some 850,000 soldiers dead, as if such human costs were not sufficiently awful, but also extends its devastation to families, homes, cities, and even nature. General Sherman on his infamous march through Georgia, with the 101st Ohio Infantry among his troops, transforms traditional warfare into an assault on the environment, destroying farms, livestock, crops, and whatever he encounters. Newton sees damage all around him. Out searching for water, he sits down beside the dangling iron abutments of a wrecked drawbridge—*burnt I suppose by the rebels*. Confederate forces also employ Sherman-like tactics. There are no rules of engagement to limit collateral damage. Company D finds evidence still ember-hot. "We came to two places where some of our Cavalry had fired … houses that morning and they were still smoldering," Beman Read reports. "They were said to be a rendezvous for the bushwhackers."

Newton can't avoid almost daily lessons in compassion. Women and children suffering from the horrors of war do not belong, I suspect, among the sights that Newton once believed might hold unreckoned value for his future life, but he cannot look away. Company D comes upon another house and barn that Newton describes as *reduced to a heap of smoking burning ruins*. He assumes that the ruined structures belong to a suspected guerrilla, but—with winter fast approaching—he also recognizes the civilian cost of military reprisals. *It was a sad sight to see a woman & her children walking the fire & where the house had stood only that morning.*

Historians calculate that the Civil War leaves behind more than thirty-seven thousand widows and ninety thousand orphans. There are no monuments, so far as I know, to the civilians who die from starvation, exposure, and poverty when military forces set their homes and barns ablaze.

Poems rarely achieve the public impact of monuments, but they often prove better at capturing the human cost of war. Kentucky-born Alan Tate—conscious of his status as a southern poet—chooses an elegiac tone for his "Ode to the Confederate Dead" (1928). The poem, far from serving as a nostalgic requiem for the vanquished but heroic South, emphasizes the futility visible in eroded gravestones and half-effaced names, like the forgotten young soldiers whose lives and identities are forever lost. Gravestones are private memorials—personal and familial—but Tate's poem denies such markers even the power of remembrance. The Civil War emerges in his elegiac meditation as a pathetic and unwitting exercise in nihilism, which might extend as well to the unprecedented slaughter of World War I, ended just ten years before the publication of his "Ode." The figure that dominates Tate's poem, appropriate to both wars, is a pitiless funerary angel with a blank gaze.

Boston-born poet Robert Lowell, who as a young man once pitched a tent on Tate's front lawn, turns from elegiac loss to bitter critique in his New England response to Tate's southern ode, "For the Union Dead" (1964). Lowell first reads it publicly at a Boston festival in 1960, and the timing is significant, as the poem appears when the Vietnam War is drawing serious protest and when student activists are pushing civil rights demonstrations into the Jim Crow South. Lowell's poem too addresses more than one struggle. Although its critique extends to multiple modern failures, its specific subject is a Civil War monument on the Boston Common—known as the Shaw Memorial (Figure 16).

CIVIL WAR *Duet*

The celebrated American sculptor Augustus Saint-Gaudens created the Memorial to honor Colonel Robert Gould Shaw and the 54th Regiment of the Massachusetts Volunteer Infantry. The unveiling, in 1897, features a parade with veterans of the 54th Regiment, a seventeen-gun salute from warships in Boston harbor, an answering twenty-one-gun salute on the Common, and a brass band belting out "Battle Hymn of the Republic." It was, as installations go, a big deal.

Art historians today rank the Shaw Memorial as among America's finest monuments. Aesthetics aside, it proves truly distinctive because the 54th Regiment of the Massachusetts Volunteer Infantry is all-black: in fact, it is the first all-black regiment raised in the North. As the poem begins, Lowell represents the current neglect of the monument in a mass of equipment that blocks his view, as the city builds yet another parking garage. The Memorial seems almost forgotten in the drive for modern progress. Saint-Gaudens was the opposite of forgetful. He worked on the Memorial for some fourteen years, even (for realism) hiring African American men as models. Realism may also explain why Saint-Gaudens puts Shaw in the central position, on horseback, seated high above the black foot soldiers. Like all officers in black regiments during the Civil War, Colonel Shaw is white.

The Memorial appropriately aggrandizes Shaw, its namesake, but Lowell sets out to readjust the lens. He does not mention the large, ambiguous, angelic figure who floats just above Shaw—perhaps a personification of Peace—and he ignores Saint-Gaudens's allusion to a well-known painting of Napoleon on horseback. Instead, Lowell's readjustments subtly undercut the heroic focus on Shaw. In transcribing a Latin motto on the pedestal, Lowell changes a singular verb to plural, so that the sentiment applies beyond Shaw to the entire regiment. More important, he undermines the spatial stasis that freezes the march in an immutable bronze stillness, as if immortalizing the regiment or perpetuating its memory in a changeless posture of military resolve. Poetry permits more fluid engagements with time than sculpture usually allows, and Lowell as poet chooses to focus attention on what happens after the frozen moment.

"Two months after marching through Boston," he reminds us as time resumes its flow, "half the regiment was dead."

A personification of Peace on the Shaw Memorial would represent wishful thinking. The dead include Colonel Shaw, killed in 1863 leading his troops in South Carolina on a doomed, suicidal charge to the parapet of Fort Wagner. The losses to the entire 54th Regiment are staggering: 272 dead. It was no doubt galling to Lowell that the pedestal of the Shaw Memorial contains opiate-like verse composed by his nineteenth-century kinsman, James Russell Lowell: "death for noble ends makes dying sweet." Sweet dying—as if it were consolation to the dead black soldiers—is not a concept that Robert Lowell is prepared to endorse. Two world wars and too many parking garages have changed the scenery. In a daring loop spiral, he links the Shaw Memorial with contemporary racial prejudice that might find its national symbol in Boston during the 1960s, with its segregated schools, all-white politicians, and a reputation for antagonism toward blacks.

"Their monument," Lowell writes, "sticks like a fishbone / in the city's throat."

Monuments—in a lesson we might draw from Lowell's poem—are always open to reinterpretation. They do not enshrine a single meaning. We can wrap them in new contexts, we can change how they speak to us, we can speak to them differently. We can see them differently. The Shaw Memorial today can remind us that forty thousand African American soldiers died during the Civil War, although the reminder constitutes a contemporary reinterpretation. The bravery of Shaw's troops, under withering fire, proved crucial to the Union cause because it debunked the racist military myth that blacks make poor fighters. It sparked the formation of additional black regiments that helped tip the balance of power. Lowell's poem too provides a reinterpretation that debunks or at least unmasks national myths of racial equality and of military glory. The meaning of any monument remains open to the flow of history and time. We are, for our own generations, the keepers and the restorers of meanings.

Glory is an award-winning 1989 film dramatizing the courage of the black soldiers in the 54th Massachusetts Regiment. Their bravery is not in question. There is no glory, however, visible in Matthew Brady's stark black-and-white Civil War photographs showing rigid corpses lying twisted and abandoned on desolate battlefields. The photographs too stick in the throat.

Newton has no time for sculpture or poetry. The book he carries with him is the Bible, which, he says, fits in his pocket and goes with him on marches, *so that I can take it out and read it when we halt a little while.*

A Bible-reading soldier, a more common sight in the nineteenth century than today, might conjure up the modern image of a closet pacifist—or perhaps a Cowardly Lion hiding behind religion—but Newton finds no inherent contradiction in carrying both a rifle and a Bible. "I have read His fiery gospel writ in rows of burnished steel!" So runs a typical line from the stirring Civil War anthem "Battle Hymn of the Republic," first published in the *Atlantic Monthly* in 1862. Newton takes pains to emphasize not only his dedication to duty and his willingness to fight but also his physical stamina as a soldier. He admits that he stops once during the infamous and exhausting Kentucky march, although only for half an hour and not because he is unfit. In the privacy of a letter home he knows that his sense of pride

LIFE ON THE ROAD

won't be misinterpreted as boasting.

While the strong ones fell out & were left sick on the road by scores & hundreds even, I never fell behind for not being able to travel.... I never asked to be excused from any duty for being unwell, no not from the day I first went to camp at Monroeville. I don't believe 4 men in the company can say as much.

Newton has seen his first battle, but he may not yet fully understand how quickly life can turn, on the road.

Confederate monuments, memorials, and memorabilia have maintained a public presence for decades on the American scene without significant protest. They survived the civil rights marches of the 1960s as if covered with a cloak of invisibility. In 2015, however, a white racist murders nine black parishioners after a prayer meeting at the historic Emanuel African Methodist Episcopal Church in Charleston. The governor of South Carolina, Nikki Haley, soon issues orders to remove the Confederate battle flag from the state capitol dome. The flag, a remnant of the white racist South, at last comes down, despite significant resistance. The monuments to famous Confederate generals, however, continue to stand nearby, like permanent features of the landscape. Rocks, trees, statues. Astonishingly, such somnolent and apparently invisible Civil War figures soon spring to life, or so it seems as they animate lively debates and heated clashes. They exit the status of inanimate objects to emerge as symbols that no longer gesture harmlessly toward a remote past but rather stir up controversy and reopen the wounds of contemporary race relations.

Donald Trump in 2016 achieves a thin Electoral College victory to become the forty-fifth president, while decisively losing the popular vote. His bullying tactics, sexist behavior, hypocrisy, and well-documented lies prove less damaging than his willingness to play upon anti-immigrant sentiment and racial fears. He maintains a base of support by tapping into white fears and resentments dating back long before the Civil War—now revived as many people feel lost in the transition to a global economy and a digital culture. Far from silent or inert, the Confederate monuments in Virginia play a prominent role in the drama surrounding Trump's rise to power. In August 2017, right-wing protestors assemble in Charlottesville to oppose the city's decision to relocate a statue of General Lee. Thugs with a racist agenda escalate the protest into a two-day riot. Lee's monument not only springs to life but also gives Trump an occasion to reinforce his support among white supremacists.

Should we blame the monuments? Tear them down, like the Berlin Wall, as an offense against freedom? Tuck them away in a museum? Surround them with explanatory plaques? The removal of a Confederate monument will not remove racism, but perhaps it is the right statement to make about the misuse of public lands. We are responsible for choosing the figures who represent us in Congress. Shouldn't we choose what figures are worthy of representation in our parks and civic buildings? A democracy honors many voices—but not the voices of racism. What should we do?

Approximately 179,000 African American soldiers wear the Union blue during the Civil War—and some 40,000 black soldiers die. Black soldiers and white soldiers both fight and die to end slavery, and today their struggle in opposing white-supremacist racism requires continued full support. The Civil War monuments, while they refer to a regional Southern past, belong more importantly to the present and future. Yes, the monuments have been adopted by white supremacists as a rallying point. There is no formula for avoiding conflict with racists and bigots. Decisions about public images linked to the Confederacy, however, should reflect a democratic consensus that embodies the core American values of liberty and justice. Can't we forcibly retire monuments much as we retire lazy, racist, and offensive politicians? Jim Crow segregationists and right-wing Trumpian crypto-racists cannot be permitted to define the future. America has a troubled history concerning race—a history we are slowly coming to terms with—and the controversies over Confederate monuments provide a useful occasion to reaffirm our respect for everyone, black, white, Native American, and other, who opposed slavery and opposes racism.

The New York City draft riots illustrate how racism, inequality, and bad law produce lethal violence. In 1863, with the defeat of Union forces a real possibility, Congress passes a law that makes all men between ages twenty and forty-five liable for military service. This draft law includes a loophole favoring the rich. You can buy your way out of "mandatory" military service for three hundred dollars. Three hundred dollars in 1863 is a sum off-limits to the poor, and police enforcement of this clearly discriminatory law brings on the most destructive civil uprising in the history of New York City. During four long days and nights in July 1863, poor white urban workers (predominantly Irish) launch a violent resistance. The real question is not why. We should ask instead how a draft riot—fueled by economic inequalities, political grievances, and police enforcement—turns into a race riot.

The unfairness of the draft law, while sparking the riots, cannot account for the racist violence that ensues. Throughout the city, white rioters assault blacks. Various buildings and two Protestant churches are set aflame, but the rioters are not indiscriminate. They lynch blacks, they burn down homes owned or inhabited by blacks, and they set fire to the Colored Orphan Asylum. The racist violence extends even to the homes of whites known to sympathize with blacks. The mobs grow so violent that Lincoln—in order to restore peace—sends federal troops to New York City that were just recently engaged in the Battle of Gettysburg.

The Emancipation Proclamation issued eight months earlier, in January 1863, may have prompted fears of unemployment among poor white immigrants. New York City sees a sudden influx of newly freed and unskilled blacks looking for work. The draft riots, however, turn into a murderous conflict in which jobs prove less inflammatory than race. The indirect evidence is clear. As the fires still smolder, black residents abandon the city, many moving to quasi-rural Brooklyn, and soon the black population of New York City plummets to its lowest level since 1820.

Racism may be ineradicable—if even a few bigots remain in its grip—but it is not invincible. Success in overcoming the heritage of slavery requires courage, and, happily, we have encouraging success stories to draw upon. Mitch Landrieu serves as mayor of New Orleans from 2010 to 2018, and during his tenure the city's Confederate monuments suddenly ignite a fierce controversy. Jefferson Davis and Robert E. Lee—or at least their public simulacra—in effect spring to life. White and born in New Orleans, Landrieu is called to preside over a bitter debate about their fate. The ensuing political and civic battles include death threats and armed violence in a divided city that Landrieu describes as "a bubbling cauldron of many cultures." The city ultimately opts to remove the monuments, but the decision immediately runs into race-based obstacles. Contractors refuse to bid on the jobs, or else drop out after vicious social-media attacks. Vandals firebomb the car of a lone cooperative contractor. Landrieu persists, however. Despite firm opposition from a majority of whites, New Orleans succeeds in removing its Confederate monuments, and

LIFE ON THE ROAD

on the occasion of their removal Landrieu delivers a forward-looking speech. "Unlike when these Confederate monuments were erected as symbols of white supremacy," he says, referring to the dark legacy of Jim Crow, "we now have a chance to create not only new symbols, but to do it together, as one people."

Landrieu is right. The monuments are symbols, like it or not, not simple bronze or marble representations of Confederate dignitaries. Powerful symbols, as any poet knows, rarely lend themselves to a single meaning, slipping toward an indeterminate play of implications. We need not only new symbols that embody aspirations for reconciliation and racial harmony. We need to reframe or remove old symbols loaded with implications of white-supremacist racism. Wise leaders and courageous citizens can help us succeed in moving toward a society that honors racial justice. It would constitute a mysterious irony if the Confederate monuments—Jim Crow symbols of white-racist hate—serve, through the discussions they evoke, to help unify blacks and whites. The New York City riots stand as a model of injustice and racism: smoldering ruins, three hundred people injured, one hundred dead, and a black population fleeing the city. The draft riots spoke then in the mute street language of violence. Today, the Confederate monuments speak to a need for new symbols, new dialogue, and a new resistance to all acts and remnants of racism.

Never let your selves worry about me. I trust in Jesus who said The hairs of your head are all numbered.

Newton's letter home emphasizes his faith in an omniscient, providential, paternal God. His all-seeing, all-knowing Father is thus unlike the detached rational watchmaker God worshipped by contemporary Deists. He knows that his family will recall what Jesus says (Matthew 10:28) before the passage about numbered hairs: "fear not them which kill the body, but are not able to kill the soul." The immortal soul is always present in Newton's thoughts about death, and he believes that God is watching over him, maybe delegating a guardian angel like the figure hovering above Colonel Shaw. Matthew is clear that God directs the lives of even the least consequential creatures, so it is not even a question whether he also cares about us. "Are not two sparrows sold for a farthing? and one of them shall not fall on the ground without your Father."

I remain puzzled by the biblical talk of hairs and sparrows. I prefer to think of humans and sparrows as co-participants in a network of mutually interdependent ecosystems that have evolved over eons. My preference, I admit, offers little solace to someone standing picket duty alone in the midnight Kentucky woods. Biological evolution leaves me exposed to the whims of improvising gene pools and to the random accidents of history. No respectable watchmaker would overpopulate the planet with eight billion human consumers. Without a coherent theology or a belief in immortal souls, I'm a pagan-zen convert to loving kindness and to the approach that activist Paul Watson attributes to an ancient Japanese military theorist: "the plan of no plan."

Improvisation, while not a source of comfort, is at least not a source of *false* comfort. It puts a premium on attention and agility, which are useful traits if you replace the fiction of a master plan with the commitment to a changing, ad-lib, on-the-road life. I wanted a life rather than a career. A career implies plans and settled paths: a map for the future. Divorce convinced me that I had overvalued foresight. Things just didn't turn out as I planned. Ever since, I've embraced a zigzag path. Maybe, if we set religion aside, an improvised life (as distinct from a professional career or settled plans) is something that Newton and I would tentatively agree on.

Although I admire the fellowship and social support that churches provide, churches are organizations, and I like to keep a safe distance from most organized adult activities. Mystical interconnections with the air and sea and sky do not require passing the collection plate. Earth-centered mundane wonders such as sunsets, seascapes, and full moons are miraculous enough, and I don't need religion in order to live by a personal code of ethics. Thomas Jefferson—a rationalist to the core—composed an abridged version of the New Testament that omits all the miracles, but it's a tad too rational for my taste. I agree, however, when he states in *Notes on the State of Virginia* (1782) that "it does me no injury for my neighbor to say there are twenty gods or no God. It neither picks my pocket nor breaks my leg." I like this laissez-faire religious tolerance, although Jefferson may underestimate the zeal of some neighbors to break legs and pick pockets in the name of their white-supremacist God.

Eros is my preferred non-god, a rough and primal terrestrial force closely allied with desire, whose gifts—which include the saving gift of love—are bittersweet. While the bitterness can't be avoided, Eros provides me with an alternative both to churches and to the widespread, if often invisible, secular worship of reason. Rationalists who swear by science often decide, incongruously, to shut their minds when empirical evidence fails to confirm their preferences. Psychiatrist Jim B. Tucker in *Return to Life* (2013) describes, in well-researched, spookily convincing detail, very young children who remember their own past lives. Do the evidence and testimonies that Tucker collects amount to conclusive proof? No. Do I remember my past life, whether as Newton Brown or as anyone else? No. Nonetheless, I keep an open mind about whether some very young children—not all but some—do indeed remember past lives, although I have no idea how or why. I keep an open mind about the extraterrestrial origin of UFOs in a universe that contains billions of planets. So-called dark matter and dark energy (forces, for now, unseen) are said to make up 95 percent of the mass-energy in the universe. There's much, I suspect, that lies forever outside the limits of what human reason or artificial intelligence will discover. Newton may be right about the Book of Matthew, for all I know. Me? I'm sticking with Eros.

Tents—at last—tents! A good thing, too, because it is raining in late November. The rain breaks a long dry spell, but the weather is turning colder, and pup tents save Newton from long nights wrapped in a rubber blanket exposed to an icy rain. Along with the new tents, the term *pup tent* enters the lexicon during the Civil War. Soldiers in Company D sometimes use the term *dog tent*. Shelter fit for a dog: a rudimentary canvas shelter shaped like an inverted V—with both ends open to the weather, and no floor. Softened to pup tent, the name soon sticks, and the tents at least offer protection from the morning dew, evening rain, and late-November frigid nights. Not guaranteed protection, however. "In pleasant, or even moderate weather they were very good," Lewis Day writes in praise of the pup tent. But in a downpour? In heavy rains, Day continues, they are "little better than nothing." "In a storm," he concludes, "a pup tent stood no show."

Newton happily accepts the pup tent's limitations when it storms, but he also takes precautions. Soldiers who neglect to dig a trench around their shelter will soon be sleeping in a puddle. During a storm, even when protected with a good trench, pup tents crowded with three or four occupants can make for what Newton calls *a huddled up mess*. Soldiers sometimes carry glowing coals into the tent to dry the mud underfoot, although at some cost in smoke. Even muddy or leaky tents, however, offer protection not only against the weather but

LIFE ON THE ROAD

also against the multiple outdoor assaults on a soldier's health. After Perryville, Newton amends his report about growing fat. Now he is quite thin. Loss of weight and coughing are common but might also prove troubling symptoms. Piles of amputated limbs in your dreams are guaranteed to take away appetite. The 101st Regiment has no rest as they pursue Bragg into Tennessee. Tents, although welcome, do nothing for the digestive tract.

Half the boys in Company D are stricken with diarrhea.

Newton belongs to the large and unlucky 50 percent. Water contaminated with certain feces-borne strains of bacteria causes diarrhea and dysentery—basically the same disease, except that dysentery includes bloody stools. The camps fail badly as models of sanitation and hygiene. Latrines dug too shallow breed disease, while soldiers who avoid latrines turn nearby bushes and streams foul with excrement. The breeze around camps is ripe with human stench. Sanitation and scent aside, diarrhea is far more than a personal annoyance. Unless we replace essential fluids lost to diarrhea, the body goes into shock, and severe shock quickly leads to death. Diarrhea is no joke. At war's end, the Union army reports 1,739,135 cases of diarrhea or dysentery—with 57,265 deaths. Twice as many Union troops die of disease as die in battle. Newton probably doesn't know it, given his earlier romantic illusions about military life, but death on the battlefield is far less likely than dying on the road of acute diarrhea.

The 101st Ohio Regiment, from its original 1000-man force, loses a total of 95 soldiers on the battlefield, including 9 officers. A significant loss. Disease and accidents, however, claim another 141 soldiers, including 1 officer. This 23.6 percent mortality rate doesn't include soldiers lost through desertion or wounds. As bare facts, this record of sacrifice argues against maintaining public monuments that celebrate so-called heroes of the Confederacy. Why not celebrate instead the thousands of ordinary soldiers who disappear into hospitals—never to reappear—or who fill hastily dug battlefield pits? It isn't necessary to blow up the monuments, Taliban-style, in a spasm of iconoclastic zeal. Better to remove them from public places, quietly and respectfully, or stash them with explanatory details in appropriate museums.

The often-maligned capitalist marketplace might offer inventive solutions for dealing with the monuments. In June 2019, a Texas law firm placed a winning bid of $1.4 million for a bronze statue of General Lee that the Dallas City Council voted to remove from a state park. The citizens likely see more value in a $1.4 million windfall than in an old, offensive statue that not only celebrates white-supremacist values but also, far worse for tomorrow, pays them forward.

*B*lack skin is easy to recognize, whereas the secretive movement of money is harder to spot. Today omnibus legislation and anonymous shell companies offer hidden pockets for stashing or transferring shady cash, and there is cash to be made in the 1860s by exploiting the new draft law. White skin, no matter how questionable a person's character, will allow poor workers in northern cities to enlist multiple times in the Union army and collect multiple enlistment bounties. Thomas Jefferson, the quintessential Enlightenment man of reason, asserts as a self-evident truth that blacks are intrinsically inferior to whites: a prejudice that he would have to abandon instantly if he ever met Frederick Douglass. (They are born seventy-five years apart, and the distance marks a national transition from the Revolution to the Civil War.) Douglass, who works on the New York City waterfront as a day laborer after escaping from slavery, soon agonizes over his decision not to join John Brown in his attack on a federal armory to get weapons for freeing slaves. Money and race are beginning to weave a very tangled web. Newton as he marches into Tennessee has already come in contact with slaves, whose conversation greatly interests him, but he never once mentions race. Perhaps he sees only their souls. Meanwhile, cold rain continues to batter the pup tents.

DECEMBER 1862: NASHVILLE

Christmas Eve 1862 holds a surprise that has no connection with bright new Springfield rifles. Justus Newton Brown is transferred from Company D to a Nashville hospital on December 24, 1862. Army medical records do not waste words: "Absent sick in Hosp at Nashville Tenn." If diarrhea remains a problem, his sudden thinness and persistent cough give early signs of a less obvious but equally dangerous trouble. The army diagnosis: pneumonia.

Newton, no longer a target, is not out of danger. Pneumonia—an opportunistic infection that inflames air sacs in the lungs—is responsible for the deaths of twenty-thousand Union troops and seventeen-thousand Confederate troops. It kills one in six soldiers who contract it, and officers are no safer than privates. Accidentally shot by his own men at the Battle of Chancellorsville, General "Stonewall" Jackson dies not from his battlefield wound but from the pneumonia he contracts following amputation of his left arm. Pneumonia is curable now with antibiotics, but during the Civil War it often serves as the merciful *coup de grace* for badly sick or wounded soldiers, particularly for soldiers with immune systems already weakened from bad diet, long marches, and cold nights spent outdoors. The unsanitary conditions in Civil War hospitals—including close contact with patients suffering from contagious diseases such as tuberculosis and typhoid—expose almost everyone to opportunistic infections, nurses and doctors too. It's a wonder that admission to military hospitals doesn't come with an automatic sample death certificate.

Newton might understandably feel anxious over his Christmas Eve transfer to Nashville, but I am breathing easier. Pneumonia puts him in mortal danger, but it also may save his life. He would see his illness as God's will. Perhaps the hairs of his head really are numbered. Or did a strange new zigzag path suddenly open up? Newton's hospital stay means that he misses, by one week, the next major engagement of the 101st Infantry, in Tennessee, at the Battle of Stones River. The fighting commences on December 31 and continues for several days, without a clear victor. It is another horrific clash. Union casualties run to 1,677 dead and 7,543 wounded. The 101st Ohio Infantry loses 209 men killed in action. If not sick in a hospital, it is a good time to be elsewhere.

Newton's transfer to Nashville brings one more significant change. As a correspondent, he enters into a profound silence. His voice is lost as surely as if he had fallen with his comrades at Stones River. Pneumonia effectively silences him.

I have no letters from Newton during the period of his hospitalization and afterward. It will be over two years before the *Reflector* publishes his next dispatch. It will also be his last.

"Dear Wife," begins a letter from Newton's father, Justus Brown, written in mid-January 1863 from the National Hotel in Lexington, Kentucky.

Justus is waiting out a sixteen-inch snowfall as he prepares to board the next train to Nashville. He is heading south to search for his son. Fortunately, General Buell and his Army of Ohio have secured Nashville for the Union, but travel in a war zone remains an edgy business. Snow and danger are not the only obstacles. Nashville has eleven military hospitals, including separate hospitals for officers, for volunteers, and (lest we forget racial bias) for blacks. The segregation of hospitals by race and by rank narrows the search, but Justus would also discover that the largest hospital holds almost a regiment-size throng of sick, wounded, and disabled volunteers. Newton is probably lying somewhere within the maze of 996 beds, if in fact he even rates a bed—or hasn't been transferred elsewhere. It won't be easy to find him, but Justus is no less persistent than his son. Consistent with the no-nonsense salutation, Justus concludes his understated letter with a brief sentence crawling up the left-hand margin, in a perpendicular or vertical column, like a sideways return of the repressed.

"I have not heard from Newton."

The family or household, in its perfect form, is composed of free people (meaning male citizens) and slaves. So Aristotle begins his *Politics*. Slavery is an ancient practice, familiar in Greek and Roman households, but it does not always coincide with racism. Homer's *Iliad*—a foundation of Western literature—begins with the quarrel over a slave girl. Roman comedies often include a household slave, almost always represented as smarter than his master, and, from a comic perspective, slavery simply reveals the intellectual superiority of slaves. Black skin too has no intrinsic link with racism in the ancient world. St. Augustine—a founder of Western Christianity—is black. Black Madonnas, a cherished icon in the Roman Catholic Church, are found all over the world. The Black Virgin of Montserrat (supposedly carved by St. Luke) achieves such renown that Pope Leo XIII in 1881 declares her the patroness of Catalonia. Chattel slavery in the American South exposes quite different attitudes toward skin color. American slavery not only depends upon a white-supremacist ideology but also entails a corresponding devaluation of blacks, with vicious consequences. The devalued status of black slaves as mere property—on the level of livestock—permits slaveholders to treat them, lawfully, with inhuman cruelties. Slavery in the American South is a Kafkaesque machine built by whites for the production of black suffering.

The suffering of black slaves exists in a realm that I can't enter, beyond imagination, despite Colson Whitehead's searing accounts in *Underground Railroad*. Suffering notoriously takes place in a space where thought breaks down. I simply cannot grasp or understand deliberate cruelty—my mind recoils from torture—and the interior suffering of individuals remains largely unknown and unknowable. I am not the right person to analyze either victims of torture or the torturers, and chattel slavery is nothing less than legal torture. Further, while it is always specific individuals who suffer, the suffering intrinsic to chattel slavery is practiced on an entire race. My point is very basic. Full knowledge is not necessary in order to recognize suffering and to help people who suffer. We don't need to plumb the psyche in order to help remove evident sources of suffering. Just help. My rule of thumb, when experts talk about suffering, is Don't Compare. Don't compare the suffering of groups. Don't compare the Trail of Tears to the My Lai Massacre. Don't compare anything at all to the Holocaust. Don't compare the suffering of two or more individuals. Just … here it comes … Don't Compare.

If the evident source of suffering lies with a government or an ideology, you will have a long and intractable struggle on your hands to remove it. The Civil War is one such long and intractable struggle.

Slavery is an obvious source of suffering, but putting an end to slavery—through a Union victory and passage of the Thirteenth Amendment—does not mean the end of slavery-related suffering. The radioactive fallout from slavery lingers across generations. The body remembers what the mind might forget. When Ruth disappears into the haze of Alzheimer's disease and no longer recognizes me, I am suddenly free to travel, and I jump at an invitation to serve as principal speaker at a weeklong event in Australia. I also plan a post-event trip to see the remote Aboriginal rock art in northern Australia. At various preliminary tourist sites on my northward trek I join up with fellow tourists, which means that I am constantly in the company of happy young couples. Solitary, I am the one lone, unattached male. I worry about Ruth, feel guilty for leaving her alone, and fall into moments of self-pity. OK. I'm at least healthy enough and lucky enough to travel. In the far-north town of Darwin, my ultimate destination, I am signed up for a moonlight dinner cruise, on which I am of course surrounded by happy, romantic, moonstruck couples. Later, back in my hotel and ready for bed about midnight, I suffer a heart attack.

The body refuses to forget. What minds and emotions don't register in consciousness plays out in the body as illness, disability, and suffering. Slavery damages more than its initial victims. Its maladies are passed down through subsequent generations with no end in sight.

What is Newton feeling in his Nashville hospital? How does Justus feel as he waits out the snowstorm in Lexington searching for his son? I don't know. The search isn't starting off well. While Justus watches the snowfall mount, the army transfers Newton to a military hospital in Cincinnati—an ironic turn of the screw, since Cincinnati is far closer to home and doesn't entail travel through a war zone. Newton, even off the battlefield, remains a moving target, and Justus must feel worried enough to go searching. In Australia, twenty hours by plane from Virginia, I anxiously await the medical prognosis after my heart attack. How, amid ordinary anxieties of middle-class life, do we understand the suffering that a young African mother feels as she is kidnapped from her village, shipped across the ocean, and sold to a white plantation owner in Georgia? I can't know or even imagine.

CIVIL WAR *Duet*

I can't know, too, the suffering that racism inflicts on the descendants of slaves. Some suffering is impossible to *recognize* when the interior experience is translated into bizarre bodily syndromes and antisocial behaviors. There is a numbness in suffering that corresponds to the numbness of the person who inflicts suffering. It is like a grotesque dance of robots—except one isn't a robot.

The rule of Don't Compare is so basic that even a politician can remember it, although almost yearly some fool-in-office has to apologize for comparing a minor crisis to the Holocaust. When it comes to suffering, whether among individuals or groups, no matter how unreadable the outward signs may be, what's the rule again? O yes. Just Don't Compare. And the two ethical corollaries? *Do* something to help defeat racism. *Lend a hand* to people who suffer.

Colonel Leander Stem in his officer's tent seven miles from Nashville writes to his wife. Despite the dangers of travel and despite leaving their three children behind, Amanda Stem wants to visit him. Perhaps she is worried about an unspecified "injury" he has mentioned, or maybe she simply misses him more as the Christmas season approaches. They are clearly a loving couple that war has pried apart. It is December 20, 1862, as her husband writes his reply.

Leander Stem, like Newton, is a man out of place. Lewis Day describes him as "the reverse of a belligerent": an attorney by profession, a thoughtful man who has led a quiet, unobtrusive life, unaccustomed to a position of command. Nonetheless, as Stem lingers in his tent nursing the recent injury and studying books he has brought on military tactics, he knows that he has made mistakes in his most recent inspection. He also worries that his second-in-command, Lieutenant

Colonel Moses Wooster, bears him "no good will." He writes to Amanda that Wooster—a man with genuine military ambitions to higher rank—has used the unspecified injury "underhandedly" in Iago-like comments to other officers, as a means of questioning Stem's fitness to lead the regiment and as a pretext for Wooster to replace him.

"You must use your best judgement about leaving home," Colonel Stem continues in his response to Amanda's plea to visit him. His qualities as a tender husband may be in part what stokes the fears, as Lewis Day writes, that he will be found wanting in battle. Lieutenant Colonel Moses Wooster is made of sterner stuff. "I know it will be your pleasure to come," Stem replies, before hastening to address Amanda's questions about what to wear. "You must not think of making any outlay for the sake of dressing well, if you do come. You are always dressed well enough to see General Mitchell or any other General. Mrs. Seney and Mrs. Mitchell will be dressed much finer of course, but their husbands can't love them any finer or better or richer than yours does you; so never mind the togging." Wartime endearments. Eleven days later, on December 31, 1862, while Newton is being transferred to the Nashville hospital reserved for white enlistees, Colonel Stem and Lieutenant Colonel Wooster both fall at the Battle of Stones River.

Stem, near the front lines, is shot in the spine. Is it friendly fire? Confederate forces searching the battlefield to collect their dead and wounded find him face down in the mud, paralyzed. A bullet has shattered his spine. Enemy soldiers move him to safety. As an officer, he is put under the care of Confederate chief surgeon John M. Johnson. He dies four days later. "I never saw a braver man," Johnson writes later. Lewis Day concurs. "Without a military education, and devoid of any particular military ambition," he writes, "it was feared by some that in the crisis of battle he would be found wanting." Day quickly adds in defense of his fallen commander: "Not so."

CIVIL WAR *Duet*

"That things are not so ill with you and me as they might have been, is half owing to the number who lived faithfully a hidden life, and rest in unvisited tombs." What George Eliot writes in *Middlemarch* (1871–72), less than a decade after the Civil War, holds true about the contributions of Colonel Leander Stem and Corporal Newton Brown. In different ways, their service suggests that we might rethink the bitter divisions that bedevil the country today. The resurgence of racist politics makes it urgent to recall the moments of solidarity—imperfect but real—that connect whites and blacks in forms of hidden life. Such solidarity—without tombs or public monuments—is often hard to recognize, but it therefore deserves special recognition. In *The Story of America* (2012), historian Jill Lepore shows how the beloved New England poet Henry Wadsworth Longfellow, apolitical almost by temperament and insulated from abuses in the South, tallies in his daily account book the sums of money he gives to black newspapers, black schools, black churches, and especially to fugitive black slaves. Lepore notes the following entries for 1856, when Longfellow is fifty: "June 13—To free a slave 5.00; Dec.—To ransom Slave 3.00." Several years later he devotes the profits from sales of his poems to buy freedom for more black slaves. Acts of solidarity across the chasm of race constitute an important story we need to keep on telling.

Longfellow sees more than a political victory when Lincoln is elected in 1860 on a Republican platform that opposes slavery. "Freedom is triumphant," he writes in his diary. Longfellow reads allegorical significance into the conflict with pro-slavery forces, as do many white northerners. In 1863, his close friend Senator Charles Sumner—an abolitionist from Massachusetts—delivers a four-hour oration that compresses the national struggle into a succinct conflict

LIFE ON THE ROAD

between Good and Evil. The Civil War, in Sumner's view, dramatizes "the sacred animosity between Freedom and Slavery." Soldiers in both armies sing hymns around the campfire. "Battle Hymn of the Republic" is the Union favorite, written in 1861 by Julia Ward Howe and sung to the tune of "John Brown's Body," with Christianity enlisted firmly in the struggle for black freedom.

> In the beauty of the lilies Christ was born across the sea,
> With a glory in His bosom that transfigures you and me.
> As He died to make men holy, let us die to make men free,
> While God is marching on.

Howe's final verse leaves no doubt which side—in this sacred conflict—the Supreme Being favors.

Freedom or Slavery. It is a stark choice—moral and religious as much as political. Does Newton fully understand Southern chattel slavery? I don't know. Huron County certainly limits his personal experience, no matter what he learned from abolitionists. On the other hand, his time as a patient in military hospitals—where fellow soldiers his own age suffer terrible wounds, fatal diseases, and die untended on rough plank beds—can certainly expand his awareness of human suffering. It is suffering still segregated by race, according to military hospital rules, but there are other ways to learn firsthand about the suffering of African Americans.

A change enters Newton's last letter home in November 1862, a month before his extended hospital stay begins. *I haven't time to describe it, but if I live to come home I can tell you about ... a thousand other things of what I have seen of slavery, for instance & my talks with the slaves....*

"I mistrust all systematizers," writes Nietzsche, and my sister, Elizabeth, invents her own non-system in which Christian doctrine is far less prominent than her concern with social justice. Before a chunk of concrete ends her young life, she becomes an ordained minister in the United Church of Christ, a liberal Protestant denomination similar to the Unitarian Church (in which we are raised) and to the Congregational Church (in which Newton is ordained). Elizabeth's choice of a denomination has less to do with church doctrine, I suspect, than with the UCC presence at American colleges and universities. She loves her position as campus minister at the University of Maine, where she practices a personal, innovative, and feminist-oriented liberation theology. I feel particularly close to Elizabeth. My life, like Newton's, tends to gravitate around women.

Newton at eighteen, and always, lives out a family dynamic in which women remain at the center of his life. His mother anchors his spiritual life, and Hattie begins her studies for an undergraduate degree at Oberlin College along with Newton, which strongly suggests that they know each other then. Hattie most likely leaves Oberlin with Newton before finishing her degree—both have an interruptive college experience—and they stay together as husband and wife for the next fifty years. My ten years married to Dee and almost thirty years married to Ruth provide a center to my life. Ellen (my daughter) and Elizabeth (my sister) are equally important, although I'm with them less.

Ellen is with me, an accident of lucky timing or evidence of a providential cosmos, on the dreaded day when I take Ruth to the local Alzheimer's facility where she will live for the rest of her life and where I am forever only a visitor, eager to leave the depressing scene and depressed at my powerlessness to change the ever-downward course of her disease. I don't often cry, although I choke up at sentimental films: a preventive not-crying. In the elevator at her new facility, as Ellen and

LIFE ON THE ROAD

I leave Ruth behind for the first time, I break down, weeping. Without Ellen I don't know how I'd have made it home.

Martin Luther King Jr. offers a theological formula for eradicating racism: "Darkness cannot drive out darkness; only light can do that. Hate cannot drive out hate; only love can do that." Darkness, hate, and racism, an unholy American trinity, seem to find ever-new forms. Legal scholar Michelle Alexander in *The New Jim Crow* (2010) documents how the mass incarceration of black males has simply "redesigned" the racial caste system endemic to the United States. Historian Ibram X. Kendi in *Stamped from the Beginning* (2016) traces the origins of racist assumptions underlying the new republic, which elects four of its first five presidents from Virginia slaveholders, and he observes that young black American males—for the years between 2010 and 2012—are twenty-one times more likely than whites to be killed by police. As the legacy of racism lives on, we are beginning to recognize that utopian claims for online social media underestimate the oppressive use of digital technologies for purposes of spreading hate. Light has its work cut out for it—serious, inventive work extending far into the unknown, cybernetic future—if it intends to drive out the darkness of racism.

Racism has gained a powerful ally or enabler when closet racists can meet online, design strategies to flood the internet with misinformation, and (if placed in positions of responsibility) manipulate Big Data in ways that promote intolerance and oppression.

It is hardly a radical idea, but I believe that families are the best place to establish a bedrock resistance to racism. Mine did. My three brothers—Topper, Mike, and Jess—provide a steadying illumination that I depend on, all with an ethical conscience far deeper than morality. They did not always appreciate my own role in their lives. As the eldest, I was (and perhaps still am) afflicted with an overdeveloped sense of responsibility—even now taking responsibility for my overdeveloped sense of responsibility. It is a trait that regularly puts me at odds growing up with my anarchic brothers, who need no keeper and apparently feel far less burdened by a need for decorum. Decades ago, at restaurants, I would squirm as they slipped odd, cryptic messages inside the paper wrappers around sugar cubes. Today sweeteners come in tamper-proof packets, and America may owe this change to the Morris brothers' sugar-cube hijinks. My parents seem to enjoy the fun—five children teach you as parents to relax or die—but I don't. Happily, I no longer feel driven to organize my brothers, all with very successful professional lives, so maybe I have learned to loosen up and let go.

My life took on a weirdly unscripted vibe from the moment when I resigned a tenured full professorship. It's not exactly a parable of zen surrender, but resigning taught me a lot. I hope that Newton, despite our shared sense of duty, doesn't share my overdeveloped sense of decorum. We both seem to me, despite my late slide into resigned acceptance, just a tad too adult-oriented and hyper-responsible.

Newton's eagerness expressed in his letter home—*to share what I have seen of slavery, for instance & my talks with the slaves*—suggests that he is learning firsthand about race in America. This firsthand learning seems doubly significant. It provides evidence that even Union troops passionately opposed to slavery as a system actually possess little direct knowledge about slaves or their lives. It also shows how Union soldiers view slavery through multiple lenses, sometimes colored less by concerns for social justice than by a quasi-religious sentimentality. Beman Read describes for the *Reflector* an encounter with a grave marker (no more than "a rough board") that contains the carved inscription *Black Sam*. "It reminded me," he writes, "of the lines we sometimes sing in camp":

> That poor old slave has gone to rest;
> We know that he is free.
> Disturb him not, but let him rest.
> Way down in Tennessee.

"Free" here does not invoke civil rights and human dignity but makes a sentimental leap to the presumptive Hereafter. It is a leap common in Negro spirituals, where the earthly life of slaves offers no hope of liberation, so any real freedom is deferred to a white-robe afterlife. Campfire invocations of a fictive "poor old slave," however, can sound more than a bit facile when the singers are young white soldiers from rural Ohio.

Any ironic parallels between Black Sam and the young Ohio soldiers slip right past Beman. They are both displaced, "way down in Tennessee," and, although forced marches bear no relation to forced servitude, the soldiers at least share a kinship in weariness. The soldiers also know that they too may soon fill a foreign grave—but lacking even a generic grave marker. Their real fears of being buried anonymously somewhere in the alien South torment Union soldiers, terrified that their bodies may be left on the battlefield like carrion, for disposal by enemies notorious for abandoning their own dead. Before going into battle, Union soldiers often pin a note to their uniform that specifies name and rank. It is a flimsy precaution to avoid the fate of Black Sam, whose race gets equal weight with his nickname—perhaps made up on the spot by the Union troops who bury him and create the grave marker: signs of respect, surely, but also a sign of something that falls short of *fully* respectful.

"He was probably the slave of some secesh," Beman decides, his reflection on slavery coming to an abrupt stop, "and had run away to our army, died and been buried by our soldiers."

Secesh. My improvised riffs with my great-grandfather are teaching me daily about the Civil War. I've never heard the term *Secesh*, and it alerts me to the unseen social and political web that envelops Newton even in his Nashville hospital. It refers to the act of secession, of course, like the related term *Rebel*, which Newton also uses. What the soldiers in Company D hate more than secession or rebellion, however, which are political or civic issues, is betrayal. Betrayal is a moral issue, and it constitutes an unforgiveable sin committed by politicians known as *Copperheads*. "We would like to meet an army of 'Copperheads' from the North," writes Beman, identifying their most treacherous enemy. "The boys are hard on that class, and well they may be: leaving their homes and risking all, only to find that they have left a horde of traitors behind them."

Copperheads, or so-called Peace Democrats, pose a significant risk to the Union war effort. Worst of all, as the Huron County boys see it, the Copperheads in Washington are led by an Ohio Congressman, Clement L. Vallandigham: the improbable villain in a bizarre melodrama testing the limits of wartime freedom. In 1863 Union General Ambrose Burnside warns that free speech in the Military District of Ohio does not extend to "declaring sympathies for the enemy." Vallandigham, in response, delivers a speech charging "King Lincoln"—a bitter insult—with sacrificing the liberty of white Americans in his personal war to free black slaves. The speech does not go over well. Vallandigham is arrested, tried, and convicted of treason.

LIFE ON THE ROAD

Exiled to the South, the wily, indestructible Vallandigham (like a cartoon character) makes his way to Canada and—as if rewriting the primer on political chutzpah—runs, in absentia, for governor of Ohio!

Vallandigham manages his gubernatorial campaign from a hotel in Windsor where he plots to create a Northern Confederacy of pro-slave states. Democracy in America is always a full-contact pastime and sometimes even a bloodsport. Newton expresses great satisfaction when Vallandigham—in what Newton calls an *awful rebuke*—loses the 1863 Ohio election for governor in a landslide.

Newton, while he shares the widespread hatred of Copperhead betrayals, is also beginning to fill out a personal understanding of slavery as a moral offense against blacks. He has much to learn firsthand, but he is open to learning, and my own firsthand education similarly begins from a blinkered childhood. Born in 1942, I grow up with the often-reprinted children's book *Little Black Sambo*. An optimistic thumbnail racial history of the United States might be traced in its changing dust jackets and cover art. The book, set in India, tells the story of a clever boy who outsmarts several hungry tigers. It first appears in 1899, a product of the Jim Crow era, but the most offensive cover may be the 1938 Little Color Classics version I grew up with (Figure 17).

Sambo, despite the decorative tigers, might as well make his home (like Black Sam) in the American South. Who ever heard of a child in India named Sambo? Sambo, I regret to say, resembles a noxious stereotype of black children known (in white racist lingo) as "piccaninnies."

Newton and I are not alone in having much to learn. So too does Lincoln, whose learning involves knowing when to abandon the search for political compromise. He has always been "naturally anti-slavery," as he says, affirming, "If slavery is not wrong, nothing is wrong." As President, however, he initially refuses to let his personal convictions take priority over his constitutional duty to preserve the Union. At almost the same moment when Newton is mustering in at Camp Monroeville, Lincoln writes his unequivocal statement about preserving the union—no matter what the cost.

An ideal outcome, fusing Lincoln's moral principles and political objectives, would be both to save the Union and to destroy slavery, but his early proposals mainly offer short-term political compromises as necessary stopgaps for preserving the Union. He even floats a last-minute proposal for a forty-year extension of slavery (prior to a general emancipation in the millennial year 1900). Ultimately, he cannot avoid war, and the Emancipation Proclamation in 1863 frees many slaves, but still not all. Issued under presidential powers to suppress rebellion, it is unenforceable by law in states *not* in rebellion; it is unenforceable in practice wherever Rebel forces hold power; and it fails to order a universal prohibition of slavery. A presidential proclamation, without the status of constitutional law, is also open to reversal by a subsequent president. Thus, Lincoln works hard to engineer passage of the Thirteenth Amendment, in 1865, which guarantees a permanent end to slavery in America. Newton, born in a free state, may share Lincoln's earlier views that a peaceful solution represents the best hope for preserving the Union, but once war breaks out he does not hesitate. He has much to learn about the unresolvable conflict between freedom and slavery.

Newton never rejoins his regiment. The military records are incomplete but provide the outlines of a three-stage journey.

LIFE ON THE ROAD

First, diagnosed with pneumonia, he arrives at a military hospital in Nashville, where he stays recuperating through January 1863. Next, he is transferred during February and March 1863 to Camp Dennison, a few miles from Cincinnati, which includes a military hospital with over two hundred beds. A contemporary engraving (Figure 18) captures the vast scale and access to rail transportation that give Camp Dennison its strategic importance.

Finally, in April and May, military records list Newton in Kentucky at the Covington General Hospital, just across the Ohio River from Cincinnati. The army transfers him to the Invalid Corps on April 30, which suggests that he is sufficiently recovered to perform light duty at the Covington hospital. He is clearly well enough to send dispatches to the *Reflector*, but perhaps he believes that readers will show little interest in reports from a hospital orderly. Or perhaps—my fate during Ruth's protracted illness—he simply loses all desire to write. Letters home, like dispatches to the *Reflector*, seem to dry up and stop.

Newton has glimpsed terrors enough both in Perryville and in the hospital system to justify a diagnosis of post-traumatic stress disorder, but it can take many months to recover from pneumonia in the era before antibiotics. He remains assigned to the Invalid Corps for the remainder of his three-year enlistment as his condition improves. The next time he reappears in the military record he reports for duty in

Columbus, Ohio. His duties are not specified, but I can offer a guess. Columbus is home to the sprawling Union army facility Camp Chase (Figure 19).

Newton is now army-certified as capable of performing light duties, although not ready to return to combat, and his duties at Camp Chase likely involve guarding Confederate prisoners.

Some 25,000 prisoners pass through Camp Chase during the war—the Confederate cemetery there ultimately holds 2,260 graves—and prison guards are no doubt in high demand. A Union soldier serving in the Invalid Corps, although unfit for combat, is certainly capable of holding a rifle and standing guard. It is not trauma-free duty. No doubt a few Confederate graves are filled by prisoners shot while trying to escape.

Newton most likely serves as a prison guard for the rest of the war, but his life is far from placid or stable. In late July 1863 the army sends him to Connecticut, where military records show that he is a guard at the New Haven Conscript Camp. He remains there, with several related excursions as a guard, until Lee formally surrenders. Writing finally from Connecticut in 1864, Newton breaks his long silence with a one-sentence summary published in the *Reflector* that, typically, says

LIFE ON THE ROAD

everything and nothing. I don't know how to interpret its clipped, matter-of-fact tone.

I left the 101st a long time ago, being sent from there to a hospital at Nashville and finally to Camp Dennison, where my health improved so that I was able to perform light duty.

No further explanation. Silence and lost data abound. Justus Brown is waiting out the sixteen-inch snowfall in Lexington, but it's unclear what comes next. Much remains in the realm of the not-known. Well, not everything. Before the Kentucky blizzard of 1863 stops him in Lexington, Justus has to overcome a major obstacle in Columbus. The governor of Ohio tells the steamboat passengers that they can't proceed through military lines. He instructs them, as Justus reports, to "go home," offering half-price return tickets. Justus—what else should I expect?—declines the offer. With a stubbornness native to the Brown bloodline, he informs the governor that he'll proceed as far as he can. Obstacles do not faze him. Justus has already made his way through military lines aboard a Cumberland River supply vessel loaded with war materiel and accompanied by Union gunboats. Guerrilla raiders burned several supply vessels and, as Justus mentions, also roughed up passengers. With only what he calls "contaminated" river water to drink, he is dealing with (as he puts it delicately) "disease." Does he ever reach Nashville? Does he find Newton? I don't know. I have learned, after many failures, to feel at home in the realm of the not-known.

World War I with its grinding, four-year, waterlogged trench combat ends in November 1918, leaving almost ten million soldiers dead and twenty-one million wounded. As 1919 dawns on a world newly at peace but reeling from unprecedented losses, Newton and Hattie in their late seventies (married for some fifty years) move to a new home in Demorest, Georgia. Georgia?

Improvisation, I see, is a trait I share with my great-grandfather, as well as a corkscrew, zigzag life moving in and out of academic institutions. What draws Newton at seventy-five to Demorest, Georgia, in the heart of the former Confederate States of America? He serves as chaplain and assistant to the president of Piedmont College—posts that he maintains until age eighty-one.

O yes. He also works on a new house. Maybe it's from Newton that I get my pleasure in woodwork and manual labor. I once appear, thinly disguised, as a character in a novella by Pulitzer Prize-winning writer Jane Smiley entitled *The Age of Grief* (1987). Cunningly hidden under the name Philip—perhaps an allusion to the cigarette brand Philip Morris—I spend my time building bookcases in the garage. (Dee is the novelist's real interest.) Newton, nearing octogenarian status, spends much of his time, when not at the college, caring for Hattie, also nearing eighty and disabled. I recall my more than ten years as primary caregiver for Ruth—the loving vocation of my sixties—before she finally slips away. I completely miss the early signs of her illness, as when she comes home one evening in New Mexico and announces that she has just quit her job. Luckily, in 2002, after twenty years as a self-employed writer, I am able to take a position as University Professor at the University of Virginia. It's now my turn to bring home the regular paycheck. Five years later, however, the signs of her illness have grown obvious. When I realize that I can't teach and care for Ruth simultaneously, I resign another tenured position.

Newton's wartime and postwar travels make my own peripatetic journey look like a stroll in the park. The army sends my parents—and me—to Connecticut, Illinois, Michigan, Virginia, and Pennsylvania, among other stops, before on my own I make extended stays in New

York, Minnesota, Virginia, Iowa, Michigan, New Mexico, and the District of Columbia, after which I return again to Virginia and then loop back to my birthplace, New York City, where Margot and I now live. A neoclassical fondness for symmetries includes what I call my personal great circle route.

Here is a short version of Newton's postwar travels. After finishing his undergraduate degree at Oberlin College, he takes an MA degree at the Oberlin Theological Seminary. He briefly attends Union Theological Seminary in New York City, before shifting to Boston for a longer stay at Andover Theological Seminary. Then, in 1870, he embarks on his professional career as an ordained minister in the Congregational Church, where he serves for over forty years as a "supply minister." Supply ministers fill in as a substitute pastor, often while a congregation is searching for a full-time minister. His career keeps him on the move, serving congregations from Maine and New Hampshire to Michigan, Minnesota, Kansas, and Utah. I am omitting his stints as a newspaper editor in Ohio, as a proofreader in Pennsylvania, and as an employee in Cleveland at the Church Envelope Company. A photograph taken when he is a young minister displays a man of dignified Victorian self-possession (Figure 20).

In 1914, the fateful year when World War I begins, he is once again back in Ohio—as pastor for his hometown Ripley and Greenwich Congregational Churches. He holds this position until, at war's end, he and Hattie (now in their late seventies) set off for Georgia.

What occupies Newton in Demorest besides caring for Hattie and fulfilling his duties as chaplain and presidential assistant? O, not much. He also teaches a course entitled Greek Language and Literature, including selections from Homer's *Iliad*, the New Testament, and

Xenophon's *Anabasis*. Homer and the New Testament make sense to me, but I'm puzzled by Xenophon. The Greek word *anabasis* means, literally, "a march inland." *Anabasis* III-IV—the section Newton teaches—tells the story of a large Greek mercenary force betrayed and stranded somewhere in Persia. The soldiers must fight their way home through alien territory, with ambushes and further betrayals at every turn. Their perilous journey concludes with a famous literary scene. From a mountaintop, the battle-weary, homesick soldiers at last catch sight of their route back to Greece, crying out as if in one voice, *Thálatta, thálatta! The sea, the sea!*

    I wonder if the scene of weary Greek soldiers far from home holds extra resonance for an elderly professor who once comes home from a devastating, disillusioning war—only to realize that home is not what he thought it was, not quite an illusion, but unstable and shifting, no more than the place that you leave from. Copperheads, corpses, and mounds of amputated limbs may turn the concept of a settled home into fantasy, but does home then trade places with a life on the road? The open road, despite Walt Whitman's optimistic embrace, never truly *feels* like home. Perhaps home, even in a settled place, is always a fantasy and always disappoints, like the road. Fantasies of home—and their inevitable disappointments—may help explain why hobo songs uncannily ring true, or what it means for prisoners to hear the lonesome whistle of a passing train. Freedom is always elsewhere. As in the Kris Kristofferson song, fictive Bobby McGees are forever searching for the home they'll never find. The railroad, the sea, and the open road all represent the endless paths that keep Americans—a mobile people—circling back to places that never quite feel like the homes they left. There is no real arrival, only more paths.

LIFE ON THE ROAD

*I*n August 1976 I pack my new yellow Jeep CJ-5 with duffel bags, sleeping bag, and tent, heading west from Iowa City for Los Angeles. A bittersweet path with a sour backstory. Dee and I decide to end our ten-year marriage in the fall of 1975 while we are both teaching at the University of Iowa, and my world abruptly falls apart. The bitterest stroke, in a series of hammer blows, is that I miss my daughter, Ellen. She has started preschool, but now I see her only on weekends: a sudden chasm after—as a modern husband—I have fully shared the day-to-day pleasures and duties of parenthood. I feel rubbed raw, all tangled up in the dark. My one unclear, desperate thought is to get out of town, away from an ever-renewing pain, but if I leave town I'll see Ellen even less. I simply don't know what to do. A yearlong Guggenheim Fellowship breaks the impasse and pushes me out the door. The fellowship seemed such a longshot that I'd nearly forgotten I'd applied.

The Jeep is an extravagant break-up gift I give myself, neither a car nor a truck, but, like me, a hybrid. Together we make our way across the Mississippi River. I have never traveled so far west. California as destination serves as little more than a glossy cliché, but my hastily improvised road trip includes three non-platitudes. I've always wanted to see Santa Fe. No idea why. A well-traveled friend recommends two ancient southwestern Native American sites, Chaco Canyon and Canyon de Chelly. I'm attracted to threes, so the chance combination of three intermediate stops serves as a sign. Off I go. All I need is a dog and a guitar to complete the country-song, brokenhearted journey, but I'm traveling light. I struggle to say goodbye to Ellen, now about to start first grade. Most nights I make tape recordings for her—sometimes capturing the patter of rain on my nylon pup tent— and every few days I search for a post office to mail off my latest taped reading from *Charlotte's Web*.

I am beginning to feel a little better as soon as I reach New Mexico. I pitch my tent in Chaco Canyon beside an Anasazi ruin older than Chaucer. Then, leaving New Mexico for Arizona, at Canyon de Chelly I hire a Navajo guide and spend an entire day driving between towering canyon walls over the narrow, roadless strip of sandy hardpack. The four-wheel drive Jeep proves ideal for crossing the shallow stream winding through the sand-bottom. Ancient stone dwellings set into natural crevices high in the canyon walls remind me of Shinto shrines tucked into their natural settings, and Canyon de Chelly holds the same reverential spirit. As I resume my travels west, the high blue southwestern skies and ever-changing clouds work their magic art. I am still shaken but improving daily by the time I roll into the Land of Therapy. Los Angeles seems home to as many therapists as drug dealers: two ways of addressing the same fundamental psychic dilemmas. With no taste for drugs harder than caffeine, I am fortunate that a new friend at the Clark Library, Michel Nutkiewicz, steers me to a therapist at a local wellness center.

My therapist, during the course of our weekly sessions, tells me a transparent story about a knight lost in a dark forest. After hopeless wandering with a faithful horse as his sole companion, he at last encounters a wizard. There is only way to escape the forest, the wizard says. He must sacrifice his horse. The knight demurs and delays. How can he possibly kill the faithful companion of his wanderings? Finally, after an extended hesitation, all at once he turns and plunges his sword into the horse's chest. Instantly, the horse turns into a beautiful woman, who leads him out of the woods. It takes me a while, but eventually (thanks to Ruth) I get it.

The Lucky One is the pseudonym I use many years later, in my seventies, for an online dating site. Luck is the higher power I believe in, along with Eros. Eros and Luck. Both, I suspect, belong to an internal wisdom of the body—bodies as a fleshly compound of mind and spirit—that most Western fact-based systems don't know how to account for. Not a big surprise, since we don't possess all the facts, and never will. How can I explain, as a matter of pure fact, that my long, winding, heartbroken road trip to Los Angeles leads me, ultimately, right to Ruth?

Our good luck makes us who we are—perhaps even more surely than our sorrows do. No one can avoid sorrow and misfortune, but many fail to get their fair share of good luck. Good luck may be written on our faces, much like sorrow in reverse. My favorite snapshot of Ruth dates from 2008 when she is already six years into the damage from Alzheimer's (Figure 21). You would not know it from her smile.

She is relaxed and happy, outside the house we built on a hillside in Charlottesville, with a view west toward the Blue Ridge mountains that once marked for Thomas Jefferson the limits of his own westward travel. Misfortune changes her—body *and* mind—but it never crushes her spirit.

Ruth lives bravely for fifteen years with the ever-increasing debilities that come to Alzheimer's patients. The disease rolls back knowledge, unravels personality, and slowly kills the body. We navigate its losses, up to a point, with love and humor. Ruth early on prefers to say that she is "dinged," but even *dinged* she knows that she is losing skills and knowledge, until she loses all knowledge of the world we share and no longer knows me. The disorientation from a wrongly prescribed antipsychotic medication once causes her to fall and break her leg near the hip joint. I help hold her down as two clumsy nurse assistants catheterize her in the emergency room, and her half-crazed eyes say "I will kill you." There is much I'd like to forget, but I am also half-crazed myself—with grief and fatigue—not thinking clearly. Only when I finish writing *Eros and Illness* do I understand my Australian heart attack as directly linked to the long, stressed years as caregiver.

No matter. Finding Ruth when I arrive in Los Angeles counts among the very luckiest moments in a life not without scars but also blessed with saving good fortune.

JANUARY 1864: NEW HAVEN AND BEYOND

Newton is full of surprises. After two years of silence, he emerges in Connecticut as a guard at the New Haven Conscript Camp. He describes it as the *rendezvous for the drafted men of Connecticut*. His quiet phrase *drafted men* reflects a major change in war policy mandated by the infamous Draft Act of 1863, which requires each state to fill a specific manpower quota through a combination of volunteers and draftees. Volunteers are paid $100 enlistment bonuses or "bounties," although the bounty varies depending on the state and district. Draftees receive no bounties. Congress, always ready to accommodate the rich, then devises the holy mother of all loopholes. Draftees can avoid military service by paying a fee or hiring a substitute. The price for a substitute averages $350 to $400, and substitutes in large cities sometimes receive as much as $1,500.

Newton has received an enlistment bounty of $100—equivalent in 2016 purchasing power to about $2,350—payable in full at the end of his three-year enlistment, if he survives. He probably receives a $25 advance when he musters in, but he is hardly rolling in cash. Union privates earn a monthly wage of $11, paid irregularly, with a modest escalating scale up the ranks. Corporals such as Newton receive a monthly payment of $14. State regulations and federal laws concerning recruitment change during the war, especially if a major defeat dries up volunteer pools, leading to a mélange of shifting options after 1863. At least we know what Newton—who signs up in 1862—receives. Not a lot. With tuition free at Oberlin College, money certainly isn't his incentive for enlistment.

Enlistment-bounties and substitute-payoffs, as it turns out, have a curious impact on Newton's life. Opportunists, especially after the New York City draft riots, see the various bounties and fees as easy money. Inventive scams quickly multiply. "Bounty jumpers," as they are called, enlist in high-bounty districts, take their payment, and then desert—only to show up a few weeks later in another high-bounty district and replay the swindle. Scammers work together in gangs, with half the gang enlisting while the other half arranges their escape. Large numbers of poor, immigrant opportunists from New York City travel to nearby Connecticut, where they enlist, collect their bounties, desert, and then re-enlist elsewhere. Newton's guard duty at the New Haven Conscript Camp, while far less dangerous than combat, includes significant peril. Guards are the immediate obstacle standing between the scam-enlistees, fellow gang members, and desertion. Newton writes in January 1864 that the enlistees he guards are *certainly the roughest fellows I ever saw.*

The *New Haven Journal* publishes a letter found in the Conscript Camp that illustrates what Newton is up against. The letter-writer explains that by repeatedly enlisting he expects to clear at least $2,000. ($2,000 in 1864 will buy a high-end BMW in 2019.) First, however, he needs to escape. The escape is clearly a well-scripted group effort. "The guard was very light," the newspaper account runs, "numbering only about eight men, and after clearing the camp, the skedaddlers scattered in various directions, and were out of musket range before a suitable body of men could be made aware of the escape." *Skedaddle*, a term Newton too uses, enters the American lexicon during the Civil War to describe this particular wartime act of desertion. It means "to run away hastily," but the escape involves more than foot speed. The skedaddlers at the Conscript Camp—thirty men in all—begin by hurling bricks at a guard. The guards shoot back at the brick-throwers, hitting one and shattering his arm. The Minié ball adds another amputee to its accomplishments. Is Newton among the eight guards on duty? He doesn't say. There are 268,000 desertions during the Civil War, so a camp guard faces regular planned assaults, some with weapons more lethal than bricks.

What is the Trinity? Newton in 1902, as a Congregationalist pastor in middle age, poses this question as the title of a closely argued thirty-page article published in a journal of theology. The question today seems so arcane and reader-unfriendly that I applaud his nerve in posing it, although earlier generations wrestle seriously with theological issues such as free will and the personhood of God. The issue boils down to fundamental questions. Is God, as Trinitarians believe, composed of *three* separate persons, Father, Son, and Holy Spirit? Or is God, as rival Unitarians believe, only and always ... One?

Newton argues the Trinitarian position, citing the relevant biblical chapters and verse, but I'm far more drawn to his inventive psychological illustration. Psychology is then a new field—Sigmund Freud and William James are not yet familiar names, especially among professional theologians. Newton's innovation comes in applying psychological insights to illustrate the Trinitarian position. We are all, he explains, trinitarian beings. We all contain three distinct mental powers: first, *a self-directed power* producing self-awareness; second, *an other-directed power* connecting us with the world; and third, a latent and mysterious power originating in what Newton calls *an unfathomable depth or substratum of being.*

One person, in psychological terms, contains three distinct powers. God, in theological terms, contains three distinct persons with three distinct powers. God the Father is akin to our spiritual power of self-awareness. God the Son carries our spiritual being out into the world. It is God the Holy Spirit, however, that most interests Newton as he explores parallels between theology and psychology.

Our *unfathomable depth or substratum of being*—our third mental power—provides Newton with his clinching analogy to God as the Holy Spirit. The Holy Spirit, he implies, does not work through our conscious self-awareness or through our connections with the world. Instead, it works mysteriously within the human soul. Newton has no doubt about the reality of such an inner-working power although (like the Unconscious for Freud) it remains unknown to consciousness. The Holy Spirit works within the human soul much as the Unconscious works within the human psyche. *As there is more in the sea than appears on its surface, so there is more in us than we are conscious of. For every recollection of which we are now conscious, or which we can now bring up into consciousness, we have a hundred recollections hidden away in the depth of being below consciousness, and waiting to be brought into consciousness by future suggestions. We have likewise within us latent powers and dispositions, which are no less real because they are shut off from our present consciousness.* Newton writes this description of our nonconscious life well before Freud unveils his developing theories of the mind.

I like Newton's psychology better than his theology, as it suggests how he understands himself. His account of the mind must apply to his own self-understanding. He thus sees himself as more than a rational being or even an immortal soul. He also acknowledges an unknowable *depth of being*—like the depths of the sea—where a tangle of *hidden-away* recollections and *latent powers* move beneath the surface of consciousness. He never says if his wartime experiences give him recurrent nightmares. Once, however, when responding to an Oberlin College questionnaire, Newton writes that he has begun to study psychology.

I wonder if he tried out this line of argument with his son, Carleton, a Unitarian minister. Carleton designs a new church for his congregation in Montana based on the model of a classical Greek temple, where the rational design includes, among its innovations an all-purpose community center with a stage for theatrical productions. Were eyebrows raised in Montana? Something must have felt amiss. Before the cornerstone is laid, Carleton leaves the ministry for Harvard and graduate study in English. Later he becomes a distinguished specialist in medieval religious lyrics—songs from an age of faith—where the language of religion is at times indirectly or openly erotic. As a widowed professor at Bryn Mawr College, Carleton marries one of his students, Beatrice Daw, a budding poet and fellow medievalist, who pursues her own distinguished career as scholar and teacher. She is also my grandmother.

Personal concerns with religious faith run in the Brown family line. Newton's earliest known ancestor among the Browns arrives in America from Rowley, England, well known as a hotbed of Protestant dissent. Oddly, he is not listed as a passenger. A stowaway? A servant? A crew member who jumps ship? Margot brings me from Madrid a T-shirt, brown of course, bearing a phrase in Spanish that translates roughly as "I don't follow the script." *No sigo el guion*. The spirit may need a freedom it can't find in the precepts of reason.

It is through the Holy Spirit, Newton writes, that God exercises his power within our souls. Our souls then give direction to our actions, and our actions give the immaterial and invisible Holy Spirit a visible, material presence *in the world*. The fight against slavery might thus signify for Newton the material presence of the Holy Spirit acting in the world. As I read his meditations on the unfathomable mysteries of being, I think of a young man marching in the dust and heat toward Perryville, standing on picket duty for hours, bereft, with no friend to hear him except God. What *hidden-away recollections* does he carry from a national blood-letting that leaves 850,000 dead? He doesn't say.

LIFE ON THE ROAD

His response may be expressed as action in the world, in a wandering life spent ministering to parishes scattered across the land.

Newton, when he musters in to the 101st Ohio Volunteer Infantry, is 5' 8", with brown hair, grey eyes, and a light complexion. So says the 101st *Company Descriptive Book*. Modest stature seems to be a Brown/Morris family trait. A yardstick would lie flat across the heads of the four grown Morris brothers as we stand together for a photo. At 5'7" and 135 pounds, I play linebacker and guard on our high school varsity football team—in an era that allows only two substitutions per play, so most players stay on the field for both offense and defense. As catcher on the baseball team, I like the collisions when I'm blocking home plate. A certain toughness comes in handy as I grow up in the working-class steel town of Claymont. Later too it helps as I fight my way through a ring of bullying teenage pals. You don't forget walking two miles home in the dark with your knuckles bleeding. Today I prefer nonviolence and dialogue—a wiser tactic, granted, for septuagenarians—but I make an exception for self-defense and for defending loved ones. Although my last years with Ruth show that I'm a reliable and devoted caregiver, my Native American spirit animal is the wolf.

A wolf-nature inclines me toward solitude, useful for a writer, but it does me no favors in social settings, where people find me too quiet. I admit to hermit-like inclinations when I'd be happy to retreat into a cave and write, obsessively, so I take some consolation in a Buddhist parable about the hermit Milarepa. Pema Chödrön—popular modern conduit of ancient Tibetan wisdom—tells the story in *Start Where You Are* (1994). A brave, crazy loner, Milarepa lives for years in caves, meditating. If he can't find food, he eats nettles until his skin turns green, but he never stops meditating. One evening, however, Milarepa returns to find his cave filled with demons. He tries to persuade them to leave, gently, but they won't budge. He tries everything he can think of, but to no avail. Finally, he addresses the demons with a proposal.

"I'm not going away, and it looks like you're not either, so let's just live here together." At that, all the demons leave—except one. Milarepa is stumped at how to get rid of this last, toughest demon. At last, he climbs into the demon's enormous mouth and says, "Just eat me up if you want to."

The last demon leaves.

The moral: when the resistance is gone, so are the demons. Zen surrender, for Milarepa, does not imply either resignation or nonviolent resistance. Rather, it implies acceptance and compassion. Tibetan Buddhism nonetheless includes an exception in demons who employ their wild, wolf-like ferocity for protective purposes. Newton's granddaughter—my mother, Emily Brown—possessed a protective fierceness, like a mother bear defending her cubs. Acceptance and compassion don't come easy, but Milarepa shows the way. A poet, he is often portrayed with his hand cupping his ear, listening to the natural world and to cosmic harmonies (Figure 22).

This Tibetan thangka featuring Milarepa hangs above my bed: a reminder that toughness and fierceness matter only as they preserve a space for acceptance, compassion, and loving kindness. Somebody is always tougher than the local tough guy. Both high schools and Major League Baseball now seek to avoid collisions, and the runner is called safe if a catcher (without the ball) blocks home plate.

Donald Barthelme, an early master of postmodern short fiction, defines the writer as someone who, embarking upon a task, "does not know what to do." Newton and I share a trust in not-knowing. Not-knowing, you might say, is something we know a lot about. As a soldier, Newton marches into unfamiliar territory, stands picket duty without knowing where to look for an enemy ambush. Not-knowing includes a degree of anxiety. As no one is shooting at me, I can maintain a less anxious relation with not-knowing as a writer's best (if still edgy) source of unexpected breakthroughs. Something's missing. Then, suddenly, a recalcitrant sentence finds its rhythm or a paragraph snaps into focus. A figure slowly emerges from within the sculptor's marble block. Newton relies on a religious faith that supports him far beyond the limits of knowledge. It must steady him both as a soldier and in his later hybrid, improvised, career wanderings.

Newton's zigzag *wanderjahre* after the Civil War include one especially surprising reinvention: as a lecturer for the Anti-Saloon League.

Intoxication is a form of not-knowing, I suppose, often celebrated as akin to the euphoric mysteries of poetic inspiration. My father regarded alcohol as enhancing social and intellectual pleasures, as when friends meet over drinks, talk, and hatch plans. Newton, however, is no friend to alcohol, much like the settlers who carve homesteads out of the Ripley wilderness. In 1830, the local Temperance Society calls for volunteers to build a Congregational Church. The call includes a question that is largely rhetorical. "Can we raise the building without whiskey?" The take-no-prisoners reply follows immediately. "It shall be done or the timber shall rot on the ground."

The saloon constitutes a stock scene in classic western films. Directors can't seem to resist a chair-splintering, bottle-smashing barroom brawl. Outside the early cinema, however, saloons provide a symbol for public drunkenness. If the temperance movement today seems like an archaic, puritanical holdover, well-known opponents of slavery such as Frederick Douglass also openly oppose saloons. Women, well before they receive the right to vote, organize to fight the evil symbolized by saloons, even down to the demeaning pictures hung there. Carrie Nation (1846–1911) is eloquent in her pre-feminist opposition to saloons: "Women are stripped of everything by them. Her husband is torn from her, she is robbed of her sons, her home, her food and her virtue, and then they strip her clothes off and hang her up bare in these dens of robbery and murder. Well does a saloon make a woman bare of all things!"

Newton's involvement with the Anti-Saloon League may begin with a local connection, since the League is founded in 1893 in Oberlin, Ohio. More is at stake, however, than proximity. Ministers have almost a moral duty to address alcohol abuse as a source of the damage both to the souls of drunkards and to the welfare of wives, children, and extended families. Newton's work as a lecturer for the League does not commit him to the total prohibition of alcohol. He publishes a moderate but densely argued proposal for regulating—not prohibiting—the sale of alcohol. The earnestness of his argument strikes me as tilting slightly toward the crackpot, but the League in its day is a formidable power, and alcohol addiction remains a significant social and personal dilemma.

LIFE ON THE ROAD

After my father retires and the drinking at home increases, the five adult Morris children arrive unannounced to stage a formal alcohol "intervention." We had already arranged for our parents' admission to separate, monthlong alcohol treatment programs. Our anxieties—preceded by equally anxious phone calls, arguments, and bickering—are heart-pounding as we each describe to our stunned, loving, and inseparable parents how their drinking affects us. Within an hour, they agree to leave for treatment. I drive away in a semi-daze to finish a two-week teaching gig at the Penn State College of Medicine. I am not at all confident that I fully understand what we have just done.

The Morris brothers can each tell a different story about the intervention, but our differences also reflect the difficulties in understanding alcoholism. Drunkenness, by contrast, is easy to spot. Alcohol turns my father sentimental, but it turns my mother angry and hostile. Are our loving parents truly *alcoholics*? Or do they just drink too much? We have entered the territory of not-knowing. One clue: as children, we invent a refrain to initiate the evening cocktail hour—"It's dry martini time"—sung to the tune of the kiddie TV theme song "It's Howdy Doody Time." In a split decision, where I cast the deciding vote, we agree to conduct the intervention without our professional advisor. Immense risk and no safety net. My mother returns from rehab far happier. My father loved savoring the distinctive permutations of grape, vintage, and terroir. Although I never see him drink at home again, I think he never forgives us.

I learn what happens to rivers during my ten years in Iowa City when, for days, the winter temperature drops well below zero. The current still moves beneath the ice. A trust in not-knowing involves an assumption that the current is moving unseen when the visible world appears locked up and icebound. It means accepting the risk that sometimes, trusting in the not-known, you will badly screw up. Eros too comes with no guarantees. Once, after an unexpected encounter, I end up in the basement saloon of a Hamilton College fraternity house, half-drunk on beer and romance. I am extinguishing lit cigarettes on the back of my hand. An intervention might have helped, and I soon learn to curb my drinking. Not-knowing about my own weird behavior, however, eventually provides a powerful incentive to write *The Culture of Pain* (1991), which opens up an entirely unexpected, life-changing path of lectures and writing. Louis Pasteur wrote, wisely, that luck favors the prepared mind. Luck also favors minds that are unprepared but flexible and open. Love, luck, persistence, and nerve. All four. Nerve may be most important if you follow not-knowing into whatever mysterious dimensions draw you on.

The news from Connecticut is not all bad. Newton reports that he has recently seen an increase in legitimate volunteers and *a much better class of men*. The particular men whom he describes belong to *a colored regiment, the 29th Conn*: the first all-black unit in Connecticut. Newton appreciates the discipline and dignity that the new black recruits embody. *Their blue clothes suit them well, and I never saw white soldiers take more pride in appearing well.* The 29th Connecticut is about more than looking good. They serve with distinction in the siege of Richmond and—on April 3, 1865—are the first infantry regiment to enter the capital of the Confederacy. They also face their share of sorrow. Forty-four men are killed or fatally wounded on the battlefield. Another 152 die of disease. Newton may not know of their fate, as new personal anxieties suddenly break his long silence. He has one more letter to write.

To His Excellency, Abraham Lincoln, President of the United States. So begins Newton's letter dated March 6, 1865. Lincoln, by modern standards, is oddly accessible and writes a number of personal replies to ordinary citizens. Newton decides to take his request straight to the commander in chief. What request? He asks for a brief leave of absence. The occasion is urgent, he writes. *Life or death.*

Newton is vague, perhaps deliberately unclear, about whose life hangs in the balance: *one who is the most dear of all the world to me.* Lincoln might assume, as I did, that Newton is referring to his mother, born Sarah Warner Edwards. If so, she makes a remarkable recovery and lives for another quarter century. But why would Newton cloud his mother's identity with such a curious circumlocution? My brother Mike surmises—and I agree—that Newton is referring to Hattie, although we have no record that Hattie is ill. She and Newton both enter Oberlin College in 1861, and Hattie continues her studies there (while Newton is away) until 1863. A serious illness may be what prevents her from returning to Oberlin in 1864. As she and Newton marry in 1866 when Newton begins his postwar studies for the ministry, it makes sense to think that they are already close when Newton writes to Lincoln. A vague reference to someone *most dear of all the world to me* might prove more effective (as Mike proposes) than a request to visit his sick girlfriend.

A leave of absence would be noted in Newton's military record, and it isn't. Only feelings of immense anguish would prompt him to write directly to Lincoln, but Newton says nothing about heartache, and Lincoln never replies. Probably he never sees the letter from Corporal Brown. There are, however, three final lucky twists. First, Newton dates his letter one month before Lee surrenders. Thus, he soon returns home without needing an official leave. Second, Hattie (if she was indeed seriously ill) must recover. Third, Newton receives an official notification from the army advising him to address his petition for a leave of absence to his commanding officer. If Newton shares my distaste for bureaucracies, this notice would be an unmistakable sign that his education in military life has reached its limit. It is clearly time to go.

*B*eman Read takes over as chief correspondent to the *Reflector* after Newton's transfer to the Nashville hospital on Christmas Eve 1862. He continues sending reports to the *Reflector* throughout 1863, despite being wounded at the Battle of Chickamauga. At one point he explains that he has rejoined Company D only after a long illness, which may refer to his recuperation after Chickamauga. I really need to get over my antagonism toward Beman for that gratuitous water-hose report. One incident helps, since it reminds me of my childhood favorite, the Hardy Boys Mysteries. The 101st Regiment is marching steadily through Tennessee. "Next day," as Beman describes their approach to Winchester, "we forded three deep streams, but no accident happened. We reached this place about noon. July 3rd. I found Father here, which was very pleasant."

Pleasant? Frank and Joe Hardy, the boy detectives, often cross paths with their eminent father in unexpected places, but with somewhat greater enthusiasm. ("It's Dad!") Dr. Albert N. Read, as inspector in chief with the United States Sanitary Commission, might turn up almost anywhere from Ohio to Tennessee. An obituary in the *Columbus Medical Journal* credits him with establishing "soldiers' homes"—in Louisville, in Nashville, and finally "all along our army lines." Beman, promoted to Captain in 1864 and transferred to Company E, spends the last six months of the war working with the Sanitary Commission as assistant inspector general: a post no doubt obtained at his father's request. His duties range from inspecting military camps to serving as temporary paymaster, but they also include measures (close to his father's heart) designed for the "relief and comfort" of soldiers.

Beman musters out with Company E at war's end. The archive at Western Reserve College—a small school in northern Ohio where he graduates in the same year, 1862, when he and Newton muster in—lists his occupation as physician, like his father. He dies in his mid-fifties, in 1897, after what I hope is a long and happy life. Really.

There are many ways to become an American besides the accidents of birth, and one good way is to wake up. Sleepwalking through my last year at Hamilton College in 1964, I almost automatically apply to Officer Candidate School as a standard alternative to waiting for a draft notice. I take the required aptitude tests, including a brain trap featuring wonky two-dimensional box diagrams, for which I have no aptitude. Despite my problem with boxes, the Army offers me a commission. Instead, I accept a student deferment and proceed to graduate school in Minneapolis, where my medievalist grandfather, Carleton Brown, once taught at the University of Minnesota, once lived as husband and wife with his former Bryn Mawr student, Beatrice Daw, and once welcomed the birth of my mother, Emily.

The first Vietnam War protests start in 1965 with teach-ins led by the anti-war Students for a Democratic Society. I am not alone in my cocoon. Some two million mostly white college students receive draft deferments. Few of us understand that this far-off war—which Lyndon Johnson escalates with a phony congressional "resolution"—is fought mainly by the poor and the undereducated. Blacks, who make up 11 percent of the population, make up 12.6 percent of the soldiers in Vietnam, but in 1965 they constitute a startling 25 percent of combat deaths. Later, as if recognizing the looming public relations nightmare, the military somehow arranges the percentage of black combat deaths to match the rough percentage of black soldiers in Vietnam. Or maybe the change reflects little more than a statistical regression toward the mean. White protests at home grow louder when in 1969 Congress ends student deferments and institutes a national draft lottery.

In Minneapolis, I arrive at the Army induction center with a letter documenting my "permanent partial disability": a wobbly knee—thanks to an old football injury—that once sends me hobbling to class on crutches and may now save my life. The Army doesn't know about my concussions, but I am slowly waking up to the madness of the Vietnam War. I still have a great deal to learn about civil rights.

There are no black students in my schools, in my neighborhoods, or on my teams as I grow up in segregated northern Delaware during the 1950s. With one late exception. In the summer of 1960, after graduating from high school, I need to find a summer baseball team. Local 1183 is a union-sponsored semipro team made up mostly of older black players. They need a catcher, so we strike a bargain. When the games end, I slip into the family station wagon and drive off to spend time with my first steady girlfriend. Like my teammates, she comes from a different world. Her world is white, working-class, and Catholic. Religion proves more significant than social class, and we spend hours parked outside her house debating the Papal Index. (*Huckleberry Finn* finds a place on the Pope's no-no list of banned books.) We also table our disagreements in the interests of making out—much to the amusement of her neighbors, I suspect. Meanwhile, at my age and far from home, Newton guards a camp of brick-throwing roughnecks plotting to skedaddle, anguishing over the life-or-death illness of the person he holds *most dear of all the world*.

LIFE ON THE ROAD

Still in uniform, Newton writes his last surviving letter home from the pitching bow of the *Jersey Blue*. The *Jersey Blue*, idling a few miles outside New York City, is a cargo ship commandeered for military service and just barely seaworthy. The ship has just left New York harbor carrying some 250 substitutes hired by wealthy New Yorker draftees to avoid military service. Some—*the hardest class that can be found*—recently took part in the draft riots. Clearly, many have enlisted with a plan to desert. Newton underlines one passage in his letter, an unusual practice, as he explains that two of the substitutes *jumped over-board when we were in East River, but were shot in the water.*

I notice Newton's shift to the passive voice: *were shot*. It lets him avoid identifying the shooters, although perhaps multiple guards fired. I'm suspicious about a syntactic ambiguity involving pronouns: *We got one.*

Newton seems to regard skedaddlers with the same contempt he feels for Copperheads. The two deserters shot in the East River are among six escapees shot while Newton performs his guard duties at the Conscript Camp. I suspect he ultimately shoots at more Union deserters than Confederate soldiers. Aboard the *Jersey Blue*, Newton appears less interested in his military duties than in describing a recent storm at sea—*a glorious sight*, as *the waves roll and dash*. Nature seems preferable to human nature as a topic, and the syntax grows clearer. Newton grumbles that the substitutes are continuously gambling. No doubt their enlistment bounties or substitute fees make for a substantial pot. One gambler, about Newton's age, wins a sum worth today about $1,000. *Poor fellow*, Newton remarks.

Why poor fellow, if he has just won a big jackpot? No one is safe on the ship while he has money, Newton says. The patriotic spirit and anti-slave sentiments that led him to volunteer in 1862 must seem deeply betrayed as he guards a shipload of gambling scammers looking for a chance to desert. New York City at least provides urban wonders worth writing home about. He looks forward to a return voyage, presumably in a more seaworthy vessel. As for the *Jersey Blue*, which merely provides emergency transport, Newton does not waste words: *it is a rotten thing.*

I make a personal distinction between a risk and a gamble. A gamble is a roll of the dice. I'm not a dice-roller but a risk-taker. The art of risk-taking lies in knowing *which* risks are worth taking. Insurance companies calculate precise degrees of risk for particular demographic groups, but personal risk-taking defies algorithms. What individuals consider a risk worth taking will differ widely. Ezra Pound writes in the *Cantos* that failure is all in the "not done." Risk-taking involves deliberate action. It is a leap of faith, at a strategic moment, when the stakes are high and failure is only the failure to take a risk. Four times, on a laughably tight budget, I sign papers to buy a new house before I've sold the old house, against sound legal advice. It is a risk I'm willing to take because I know how much the new house matters to Ruth. OK. The fifth un-sound purchase—my condo in Richmond—is a risk I take after Ruth no longer recognizes me, a risk undertaken for my own benefit, unless risky real-estate deals are now an unbreakable bad habit.

Ruth's willingness to take risks makes us kindred spirits. I remember the day in New Mexico when she returns home and announces, with no advance warning, that she just quit her job. I don't see it as a sign of incipient Alzheimer's because risk-taking belongs to Ruth's MO.

LIFE ON THE ROAD

I envy her free spirit. I know she dislikes her careerist boss, and I'm OK with her decision to quit. She has always been impossible to intimidate. Still, it is 2002; I am sixty; and we are in immediate need of a monthly paycheck. We fly to Charlottesville on a preliminary house-hunting expedition, with no assurance of a job. Ruth goes silent during the trip, which I note but don't understand. I make a rare unilateral decision and sign a contract to build a new house in Charlottesville—naturally, before selling our house in Albuquerque— and hope that Ruth will come to like it. I also hope I'll eventually find a job and be able to make the monthly mortgage payments.

Luckily, the builder requires only a down payment until the house is finished, and at the last minute the University of Virginia offers me a job. About the same time, Ellen, who has left a tenure-track position in Wales to take her chances as an unaffiliated scholar in New York City, happily lands a tenure-track position at Barnard College. Risk-taking is a tricky business. You need good luck, and you have to understand what truly matters *to you*. Eros, as usual, is my guide.

"Give all to love," Emerson writes. Ruth and I could have adopted it as our house motto. The multiple risks we take are all for love. Then one day a Virginia state police officer arrives at our front door with Ruth and informs me that she was driving north in the southbound lane of a major divided highway. All at once, my suspicions that she has been acting strangely go on high alert. Something—I don't yet know what—is wrong. Terribly wrong.

Many changes have taken place since that September day, when we left camp at Monroeville for Dixie—sad changes, some of them. Newton writing from his post in New Haven no doubt reflects on the death of comrades. Sadness, however, does not obliterate the cheering memories of home. It is not so much a material home that he longs for. Rather, the *memories* of home are what sustain him and seem always a source of consolation amid so much mortality.

Newton, although he dies in Georgia, is buried in Ohio. Ohio is the home he leaves in order to become who he will be—in his years of wandering—and it seems fitting that his final resting place is on Ohio soil. The oddly ambivalent status of home in modern American life seems confirmed by the Census Bureau, which reports that during our lifetime we move, on average, twelve times. I am certainly a veteran of many U-Haul vans. Homer's *Odyssey*, the great Western epic of homecoming, suggests that the return home exerts an almost evolutionary pull, as if for migrating birds or salmon. The Morris home in Wilmington, with its sturdy stone walls, remains a source of nostalgia. We buried my father's ashes in the front yard. Once, years later, I saw the house listed for sale, and I considered making an offer—but couldn't afford it. So much for nostalgia. An attachment to place can also be the source of unending conflict and sorrow in a world of tent cities increasingly filled with asylum-seekers, political exiles, climate-change migrants, and erected overnight to house desperate, impoverished, mostly non-white refugees.

Newton's final contribution to the *Reflector*, written from New Haven, circles back to home less as a place than as a locus of values. *I cannot express the satisfaction I have felt, as often as I have heard from my native State and have been reassured that Ohio was still doing her duty, that her patriotism was not excelled. While I have been here in New England, I have been proud to point to the Buckeye State as an example of loyalty; and I think I might well be so after the awful rebuke she gave to Copperheadism last fall.*

What awful rebuke? The 1863 landslide Ohio gubernatorial election delivers a firm and final repudiation of the wily and indefatigable

Clement L. Vallandigham. The traitorous chief Copperhead no longer troubles the Buckeye garden of loyalty that answers to Newton's fantasies of home.

The colorful Vallandigham, despite his egregious shortcomings, offers a hopeful embodiment of change. After the failure of his Canada-based run for governor of Ohio, he absorbs several more defeats before retiring from politics to practice law. Law would seem safer than an indictment for treason, but during a courtroom demonstration—designed to clear his client of a barroom murder—Vallandigham manages to shoot himself in the abdomen. He dies from the wound, but at least his courtroom demonstration proves effective. His client is acquitted (although killed four years later in another saloon brawl). Before his ill-fated return to the law, however, Vallandigham renounces his former Copperhead views and helps win Ohio to a forward-looking policy known as the "New Departure." The New Departure aims to bury all memory of the pro-slavery "dead past" and to secure equal rights for all, regardless of "race, color, or condition." A new departure, unfortunately, can't withstand simultaneous Jim Crow efforts to resurrect the dead past, reborn as Ku Klux Klan terror and Confederate monuments.

There is more than one way to resist a monument. On a moonless night in December 1997, a commando group of young Native Americans approaches the twelve-foot bronze equestrian statue of the Spanish conquistador Don Juan de Oñate. Oñate is the founding governor of the Province of Santa Fe de Nuevo México, where he serves from 1598 to 1610. He is no hero to the native peoples of New Mexico. In 1599, after a revolt in the Acoma pueblo, which includes launching an abusive Spanish priest from the pueblo's cliff-top edge, Oñate orders his troops to cut off the right foot of Acoma men over age twenty-five. Exactly four hundred years later, as New Mexico celebrates the quadricentennial of the first Spanish settlement, the commando group deploys an electric saw to sever the bronze right foot from Oñate's statue ... boot, spur, and stirrup. Their action is less iconoclasm—the wholesale destruction of images—than a symbolic protest employing highly selective damage. Along with a photo of the severed boot, they send a written statement to news outlets that plays on ideas of freedom and fame.

"We took the liberty of removing Onate's right foot on behalf of our brothers and sisters of Acoma pueblo. We see no glory in celebrating Onate's fourth centennial...."

Monuments don't spring spontaneously from the earth. They are never innocent. The city of Santa Fe earmarks half a million dollars to celebrate the Spanish colonization of New Mexico. What do Americans today want to remember and to celebrate? What do we want to resist? In New York City, the Public Design Commission in 2018 votes to remove a statue of one J. Marion Sims—erected in the 1890s—after learning that Sims conducted medical experiments on slaves. New Yorkers remain divided about Columbus Circle and its celebration of a Spanish conquistador responsible for horrific atrocities committed against native peoples. When it comes time to rethink public monuments on public land, I have just three words of advice. Remember Oñate's foot.

Is pneumonia Newton's lucky charm? It first takes him off the battlefield. Then, he beats the one-in-six odds that the disease will kill him. The hospital too, while a scene of death and medical terrors, at least spares him from worse scenes of bloodshed and carnage. His personal beliefs clearly do not rule out violence or the use of force. He carries a rifle, and the evidence suggests that he uses it, if only against deserters. His religious beliefs suggest that he would fire in the line of duty while also recognizing that enemies and deserters possess both an immortal soul and the capacity for change. The Congregational Church (to which he devotes his life) maintains as a founding doctrine "the priesthood of believers." Everyone, they believe, has God-given access to "wisdom, guidance, and power." Everyone, even an enemy or reprobate, contains within the resources that permit changing course and doing the right thing.

Newton uses the term *ruffians* to describe the lower-class, venal enlistees and likely bounty-jumping deserters who spend their free time gambling. He clearly disapproves, but he makes a point of writing confidently that even ruffians—once sent to the front—*will prove to be brave soldiers.*

Newton would have a religious explanation for what I'm calling luck. I am using my online dating-site pseudonym The Lucky One when I contact Margot (whose pseudonym is Juliet) to ask if she'd be willing to meet for coffee during my brief visit to Ellen in New York City. She agrees—replying, with a self-confidence or clairvoyance I like, "You ARE lucky." It feels as if she already knows me, and I couldn't agree more about my good fortune. I am, despite my share of mishaps and sorrows, a very lucky guy.

*R*esurrection City. The biblical shantytown in the nation's capital, erected in May 1968, has dissolved, like a decomposing environmental artwork that sinks back into the surrounding terrain. Volunteers build the plywood-and-plastic miniature village almost overnight on a vacant tree-lined corridor stretching from the U.S.

Capitol Building to the Lincoln Memorial. Although mostly forgotten today, Resurrection City holds special importance as the last public protest organized by Martin Luther King Jr. It stands as the material and conceptual centerpiece of King's visionary direct-action rally linking civil rights for blacks with the underlying pan-racial problem of poverty in America: the Poor People's Campaign. Poverty hurts poor whites and poor blacks alike, King argues. It is corporations, CEOs, legislators, and government policymakers who suddenly emerge as the bad cops who patrol and enforce the borders of hunger in America. A campaign that promises to create solidarity between poor blacks and poor whites represents a serious danger to the status quo.

Resurrection City and the Poor People's Campaign embody an unlikely, underground alliance between Martin Luther King Jr. and Robert Kennedy. Kennedy, then attorney general and soon candidate for the Democratic party presidential nomination, urges King through an intermediary "to make hunger and poverty visible." Kennedy wants a visible image to dramatize the abstract issue of hunger in America. King delivers a knockout symbol. Resurrection City, set against the backdrop of the looming, marble Washington Monument, constructs a deliberately ramshackle, living anti-monument. It is less an object or thing than a slowly unfolding event. Fifteen mule-drawn covered wagons roll into the city on June 17. For the next six weeks, some three thousand people take up residence in the tumbledown structures adjoining the National Mall. This temporary living monument to poverty and hunger reflects a massive change in how King understands the future of race relations in the United States. "We have moved from the era of civil rights," as he describes this militant new direction, "to an era of human rights."

Just weeks before the scheduled opening of Resurrection City, Martin Luther King Jr. is shot and killed.

News of King's murder reaches Robert Kennedy—now a declared candidate for the Democratic presidential nomination—when he is in Indianapolis, scheduled to give a stump speech. His staff worries about the locale previously selected for the speech in a part of town known as poor, black, and dangerous. They urge him to cancel, but Kennedy refuses. It is raining. The audience, mostly black and hostile, includes gang members primed for violence. Kennedy mounts the bed of a pickup truck. For six minutes, he speaks straight from the heart, and he talks (for the first time ever in public) about his own murdered brother. This is not a standard stump speech. The rain-soaked crowd turns quiet. Something more important than an appeal for votes is taking place. With his speech in the heart of black Indianapolis, Kennedy fuses his political future with the legacy of King. Despite their history of mutual mistrust, Kennedy implicitly affirms King's vision for an America in which blacks and whites work together, in nonviolent solidarity, against hunger, poverty, and racism.

Andrew Young, traumatized in the immediate aftermath of King's murder, watches Kennedy's speech on television. Still in his early thirties, executive director of the Southern Christian Leadership Council and among King's principal lieutenants, Young has come to Memphis to help King organize a march in support of the striking local sanitation workers. After a long day spent fighting a Memphis court injunction, he returns to the motel where King has just been shot. Years later, after serving, as a congressman from Georgia, as the first black U.S. ambassador to the United Nations, and as the mayor of Atlanta, Young remembers watching Kennedy speak only hours after King's murder, thinking, "He's probably going to be next."

He is.

Robert Kennedy is shot just after winning the all-important Democratic primary election in California. Racial healing loses another potential leader, but—murdered just five months apart—Kennedy and King have one final point of convergence. The Poor People's Campaign and Resurrection City proceed, despite the twin murders, in the spirit of King's message of nonviolence. A poster from the Poor People's Campaign (Figure 23) makes it clear whose spirit presides over Resurrection City.

Resurrection City faces trouble right from the start, however. Incessant rain turns the dirt roads into rivers of mud. Sidewalks (no more than wood planks) prove as ineffectual as the tent-like plywood structures hastily built to house several thousand out-of-town residents. Violence makes its way into the enclave of nonviolence as the rain continues to fall. Andrew Young is right. Twenty-six hours after the news that he has been shot, Robert Kennedy is dead.

The RFK funeral procession on its slow route to Arlington Cemetery passes through Resurrection City. John F. Kennedy, Martin Luther King Jr., and Robert Kennedy all shot dead. Enough. Then the Capitol Police shut down Resurrection City one day early with a tear gas assault.

Our escape from political assassinations into the Boundary Waters Canoe Area does not last. Dee and I leave Minneapolis in August 1968 in order to take up our asymmetrical roles (faculty member and faculty wife) at the University of Virginia. Dee is soon juggling a PhD dissertation and motherhood, as we both realize how unprepared we are for Ellen's arrival, in February 1970. Beyond ordinary new-parent overload, there is no refuge from nationwide turmoil. Anti-war protests and Vietnam-inspired violence reach even to a sleepy southern university famed for its country-club ambience and gentleman-Cs. The times they are a changin'. During my spring term as a rookie assistant professor, National Guard troops shoot down student protestors at Kent State University. Mr. Jefferson's University erupts as angry students fill the stately neoclassical Lawn.

Our marriage is beginning to lose its way. Two years later, my first book unexpectedly produces a job offer at the University of Iowa, and, in a rare break with anti-nepotism rules, Iowa also offers Dee a job (which she richly deserves). We paper over the fissures and move to Iowa City—a professional advance but a personal setback. Our marriage soon fails. I feel we gave our relationship everything we could until there was no more left to give, or no give left.

Our breakup hits me like a riptide. I am underwater and gasping for air. My father and mother raise five children in a marriage that lasts more than half a century. Divorce, at our dinner table, is understood as a failure that produces "broken homes." I feel that I'm failing both as a husband and as a father. Alone in the empty house in Iowa City, reverberating with an emptiness inside me, I am inhabiting my own private Resurrection City, complete with tear-gas equivalents.

It is often said, wrongly, that 50 percent of all U. S. marriages end in divorce. The divorce rate per 1,000 married couples (in figures for 2008) ranges from 14.3 percent in North Dakota to 34.5 percent in Washington, DC. An itinerant, I fall somewhere within the national average of 19.4 percent. My distress, then, is widely shared, and I have outgrown any need to assign blame. I am thankful that Dee and I have developed—after an initial chill—an affectionate friendship, which reaches across our far-flung circle of loved ones, now with Ellen, Sev (her husband), and their extraordinary daughter, Jules, as the center. Riffing on the title of a 2002 popular film, I now happily refer to my big fat extended family.

CIVIL WAR *Duet*

As he rides the pitching bow of the *Jersey Blue*, Newton is not far from my birthplace, New York City, where I am born in August 1942. I am born into a world at war. Factories churning out tanks will soon, in peacetime, convert to automobile production lines, with penicillin and Silly Putty the latest inventions. Americans are still stunned, however, after the shocking Japanese attack at Pearl Harbor, on December 7, 1941, and the attack has a personal relevance. On December 7, 1941, Emily Brown and Tony Morris learn that Emily is pregnant. Unmarried, they spend the day walking around Greenwich Village discussing, as my father puts it in his privately published *Autobiography*, "what to do." It is clearly an absorbing discussion: "We hardly heard the announcement that Pearl Harbor had been bombed."

I am alarmed to learn only a few years ago that the discussion about "what to do" results in a joint decision in favor of an abortion.

My father, a medical student at NYU, locates a woman physician so that Emily can discuss the (then-illegal) procedure in the privacy of a professional sisterhood. How many women, I wonder, practice medicine in New York City in 1941? Luckily, the physician they locate is, from my point of view, ideal. "Why have an abortion?" she asks Emily. "You're in love with the father, who's a medical student. You'll be able to take care of the baby. Go ahead and have the baby!"

Whew! Thanks, doc. Emily and Tony, I'm relieved to say, make the right decision. (Right for me and right for them: I support a woman's right to choose, although I'd like to see abortion as a rare last resort.) They get married, I get a voice, and I know how to use it. At his graduation from NYU medical school, my father looks out at the assembled audience but can't locate his family. Then, during a lull, he hears a child's voice pipe up. "Ice cream!" "I knew then," my father writes, "that at least David had made the ceremony." I still dislike academic ceremonies—I miss them whenever possible, including my own—and I still like ice cream.

LIFE ON THE ROAD

Tony soon accepts a residency in Delaware and practices medicine in Wilmington for some thirty years. Colleagues describe him as a "doctor's doctor"—the doc to whom doctors send their families—but his medical expertise is the smaller part of what interests me here. Still segregated in the 1960s, Delaware carries over its racial division from schools into medical care. In a direct response to the murder of Martin Luther King Jr., Tony becomes the driving force in creating a new, free medical clinic opened in a black neighborhood of downtown Wilmington called Southbridge.

SMAC—short for Southbridge Medical Activities Committee—comes into existence as an idea hatched one evening at the Morris home as Tony and Emily meet with a few close friends. The Southbridge community is not so much *under-served*, in the cold language of policymakers, as completely *un-served*. Access to medical care is as scarce as local pharmacies. The friends appoint my father as ringleader. His job is to engage a local hospital administrator in discussing their proposal for a free clinic, which leads to more discussion. Many months later—with several key financial donations—their idea takes material shape in Southbridge. White doctors (almost a redundancy then) donate their time to provide no-cost medical care for mostly black patients. Patients come in the evenings, when the doctors are free to volunteer and when

patients won't lose time at work. Despite a prominent notice stating that there are no drugs on the premises, a break-in soon occurs at the "facility"—two narrow row houses tacked together beneath a clapboard facade—identified by block letters above its front door as the Southbridge Medical Activities Center (Figure 24).

Nothing is taken. The break-in looks like an inverted form of neighborhood watch. The patients are watching the doctors.

The white, middle-class, professional organizing group does not know that SMAC—spoken aloud as "smack"—is 1960s street slang for heroin. Once informed, they accept their not-knowing with chagrin and good humor. The name sticks. Its two meanings imply a meeting of divided worlds—white doctors, black patients—with a promise larger than anyone knows.

Today, expanded and renamed the Henrietta Johnson Medical Center, the free clinic formerly known as SMAC belongs to a network of federally funded community health centers. It has grown to include branches in two locations in the greater Wilmington area (Figure 25).

The Henrietta Johnson Medical Center has no need to remember the initial SMAC organizing committee or the circle of white friends, mostly doctors, appalled at the murder of King and searching for an appropriate way to respond. Like Resurrection City, it is a living monument, and it depends for its impact on slipping almost unnoticed into the daily life of its environment. "We are here to serve our community and ensure better health for our patients," as the website proclaims in 2019, "regardless of their ability to pay."

There is a lineage, or perhaps a jagged trajectory, that connects people across so-called racial lines. It is a trajectory we should not lose

LIFE ON THE ROAD

sight of simply because it's hard to recognize. The horrific slaveholding past does not tell the whole story of changing race relations in America. Racism, while seemingly impossible to eradicate, calls forth resistances, remedies, solidarities, and hard work. Tony, describing the origins of SMAC, writes that there is an unending stream of weekly meetings with a changing cast of characters ("among whom I was nearly always a player"). The logistics and economics are complex. Representatives of the black community hold prominent positions both on the SMAC board and in the daily operations, from the outset. The African American nurse available during the day holds the patchwork clinic together. Decent health care is a matter of civil rights, but it is also a just and basic human right. "The arc of the moral universe is long," King declares, "but it bends toward justice."

Iconoclasts in Richmond are frustrated. No statue gets blown up or trucked off at night to the dump. The Monument Avenue Commission issues its 115-page final report in July 2018. Over eleven months, the ten-person distinguished commission holds public meetings with some twelve thousand attendees and receives some eighteen hundred letters or emails. Ultimately, it recommends leaving in place the four Confederate generals on horseback, while removing the statue of Jefferson Davis. Some critics view the report as a whitewashing, weaseling failure to do the right thing, by which they mean "remove or destroy" the statues, but I think it offers a valuable precedent for interracial dialogue and cooperation.

The commission recommends two specific changes in addition to removing the statue of Jefferson Davis. First, it recommends employing various media—from printed texts to video games—to explain the history and significance of the monuments. Second, it recommends adding *new* monuments. As one example, it recommends adding a memorial to the United States Colored Troops. The USCT includes some 175 regiments—mostly African American soldiers—who, at the war's end, make up 10 percent of the Union army. "I do believe the recommendations of the Monument Avenue Commission are actionable," Mayor Levar Stoney remarks as he accepts the report, "and something that can serve as a foundation for reconciliation or healing here in the city."

Reconciliation and healing, as an ongoing, unfinished process, strike me as far more important than the fate of a Confederate monument. The choices should focus on the best available means to reconcile and to heal. Moreover, I see no single right answer to the question of what to do with Confederate monuments. It is, as college teachers put it, an essay question. Some public decisions are tangled up in legal issues. Virginia laws concerning war memorials, for example, prevent unilateral decisions by local officials. Local voices expressed as votes are needed to repeal regressive laws. A productive dialogue also needs to include more than local voices. The National Endowment for the Arts has funded an international design competition to "re-imagine" Richmond's Monument Avenue. Such collaborative efforts help widen the range of voices, engaging national and international perspectives on racism and racial injustice. A single "stupid" monument—as Charles Barkley puts it—can serve to initiate a large and important discussion of human rights. Mute statues are inert, no matter how noxious or offensive their origin, but racism is an active toxin. Racism, racial injustice, and the hatred promoted by white supremacists are what we need to overcome, in a persistent, principled extension of the Civil War. Confederate monuments can serve a valuable unintended purpose if they contribute to reconciliation and healing, whatever we the people finally decide to do with them.

LIFE ON THE ROAD

Persistence, I used to think, is a trait I inherited from the Morris line of Nova Scotia sea captains, but now I'm wondering about the Browns. My mother, born Emily Brown, is incensed that her children on their daily walk to school in Claymont have to cross a busy highway with no traffic light. Her letter to the editor proves futile. Undeterred, she organizes a small group of concerned mothers. They clasp hands, wade into the traffic, and create a car-stopping human chain. She ensures that a friendly photojournalist just happens to be passing by. A stoplight soon appears. Equally persistent in opposing the Vietnam War, she mounts a weekly vigil outside the U.S. Courthouse in Wilmington. Her determined protests often draw taunts from the lunch crowd at the fashionable Hotel DuPont, but she persists. If her persistence connects me with the line of Brown religious dissenters, I likely owe an optimistic temperament to the Morris line of seafarers, who endowed my father with an invincible internal buoyancy that I too apparently inherit.

Montaigne once wrote that to philosophize is to learn how to die. "I have tried in my time to be a philosopher," Oliver Edwards explains to his philosophical former classmate and moralist, Samuel Johnson, "but, I don't know how, cheerfulness was always breaking in." My invariably cheerful father makes what I regard as a wise, if unphilosophical, decision when he replaces his cramped, flimsy, two-seat 1958 Nash Metropolitan—possibly the worst automobile Detroit produced in its long history of misfits. The replacement? A brand-new all-white 1964 Ford Falcon convertible. He drives to his office each morning with an almost visible pleasure, top-down even in winter. As a college senior, I am not above asking to borrow his prize—a huge dating upgrade over our boxy VW Microbus. On a return trip from upstate New York, I hit a slippery patch and skid into a bridge abutment. The Falcon limps home with a leaking radiator and a crumpled front grille. I expect a stern reprimand. My father—as we survey the damage—says simply, "You're safe. We'll fix it."

It will be hard to defeat racism without persistence, optimism, and an openness to the not-known, which may prove more reliable than any one plan. The avant-garde musical composer John Cage at sixty-five exhibits a portfolio of art prints entitled *Seven Day Diary*, completed during a one-week crash course on etching: "an activity," he tells an interviewer, "that would be characterized by the fact of my not knowing what I was doing." Knowledge comes in handy at times (say, if you want to send a spacecraft into lunar orbit). I don't devalue knowledge, but I think we often overvalue it. We also need, at least as a supplement, an optimistic resilience that allows us to persist despite what we know about the human capacity for ignorance and evil. Cage seems to agree. The interviewer asks what the advantage is in not knowing what you're doing. In full zen mode, accepting both unknown forces at work in the universe and the limits of knowledge, Cage replies briefly, "It cheers up the knowing."

Newton Brown completes his mission on the *Jersey Blue* and returns to New Haven with a shipload of roughneck enlistees looking to desert. Meanwhile, the 101st Ohio Volunteer Infantry, without Newton, without Beman Read, without George Drake, and without Leander Stem, fights on through the corpse-ridden war that ultimately kills 2 percent of the U.S. population. Newton, after Perryville, is spared witnessing the death of comrades, but he also misses the unpredictable wartime flashes of courage and spirit.

"Take that hill, Kirby!"

LIFE ON THE ROAD

Captain Isaac M. Kirby receives command of the 101st Infantry on the death of Colonel Stem, and (promoted to colonel) he remains in command until the end of the war, when he is elevated to the rank of brevet brigadier general. He also becomes a legend among soldiers of the 101st Regiment. In December 1864, as the two-day Battle of Nashville rages on, General Nathan Kimball sees an opportunity for a breakthrough. "Take that hill, Kirby!" he orders. "I'll do it," Kirby replies. And he does. "I'll do it" always draws a smile among veterans of the 101st Ohio, who fight on, bravely, in the crucial Union victory at Nashville and later as they pursue the retreating Confederate army further into the South.

In mid-March 1865, the Huron County boys—what's left of them—are making camp in Alabama when orders come to undertake a dangerous new mission. With their I'll-do-it spirit, they leave Alabama and relocate somewhere in the mountains of North Carolina—when news suddenly arrives about the fall of Richmond. The endgame is approaching, after three long years of marching and fighting. Emotions explode as more news arrives announcing Lee's surrender. "Every face beamed," Lewis Day reports: "every step was young—patriotism and enthusiasm fairly sizzled."

Then shock. Five days after Lee's surrender, Abraham Lincoln is murdered.

Shock turns to anger at reports that Lincoln's assassin is a Confederate sympathizer. "Involuntarily and from force of habit," writes Day, "the boys looked to their arms." Enraged, they are "once more ready to face southward. But"—as if Day's bland, everyday conjunction could express exhaustion, resignation, and the sense that a new, unknown order of time has just begun—"the war was ended."

CIVIL WAR *Duet*

The war is over, but not the suffering, not the legacy of racist hate. Heartbroken, Walt Whitman mourns for the nation as much as for its fallen president. The death of Lincoln evokes one of his most celebrated poems—"O Captain! My Captain!"—in which the captainless ship of state faces a deeply uncertain future:

> But O heart! heart! heart!
>   O the bleeding drops of red,
>   Where on the deck my Captain lies,
>   Fallen cold and dead.

The lines seem to stagger down the page with the thought-destroying blow. Whitman never recovers the optimistic voice of his prewar writing, when he embodied the promise of an all-embracing democratic plenitude. The regressive southerner Andrew Johnson, a states'-rights Democrat, follows Lincoln as president for the next five years, barely surviving by one vote removal from office. The war is over, but not the discord, not the recriminations, not the sorrow. What, if anything, has the vast bloodletting taught us?

"The lesson that our war ought most of all to teach us is the lesson that evils must be checked in time, before they grow so great."

The speaker is Harvard philosopher and psychologist William James. He is speaking in Boston—thirty years after Lee's surrender—at the dedication of the Shaw Memorial. James, fifty-five, has a personal stake in the lesson about stopping evils. His younger brother Garth "Wilky" James, a committed abolitionist, enlists at seventeen and fights with Colonel Shaw's 54th Massachusetts Regiment in their doomed, futile assault on Fort Wagner. Wilky there suffers terrible leg wounds that torment him ceaselessly afterwards and likely hasten his death at thirty-eight. The evils that as a nation we fail to check in time, as William James can attest from personal experience, will recoil upon us with heart-breaking personal consequences.

LIFE ON THE ROAD

In 1864 William James begins medical studies at Harvard after a variety of physical and psychological maladies—from neurasthenia to suicidal depression—keep him out of uniform. His essay "The Moral Equivalent of War" (1910) bravely seeks to understand the positive psychological side-effects, for individuals and societies, that make warfare so hard to eliminate. Earlier, however, James sketches his brother Wilky convalescing at home, with eyes closed and mouth agape, as if pain has pursued him even into sleep (Figure 26).

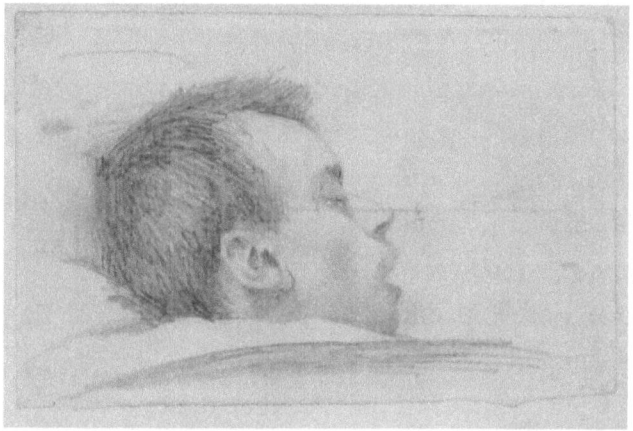

The drawing belongs among the basic lessons that James draws from the war. A firm, timely opposition to evil is necessary to prevent more lives being wasted, as Wilky's life is wasted, in an immense, unknowable, and ultimately preventable suffering.

Newton Brown musters out—in Cleveland—on June 21, 1865. It is the day of the year with maximum daylight—the same day, may years later, when a chunk of errant concrete kills Elizabeth. The Army pays him $19.62 in a clothing allowance plus $75 due from his original $100 enlistment bounty. The war has sent him by foot, by rail, and by ship into Kentucky, Tennessee, and Connecticut, then to (or just outside) New York City, and finally back again to Ohio. It sets the pattern for a much longer journey, with stops in Wisconsin, Maine, Michigan, Kansas, New Hampshire, Minnesota, Alabama, Massachusetts, Pennsylvania, Utah, and Georgia, which might well be called, without undue exaggeration, a semiprofessional life of wandering.

Wandering—from an ancient root meaning "to turn or weave"—takes its rhythm for Newton not from idleness, aimlessness, or indecision. He is not a drifter. He holds positions as professor, minister, lecturer, administrative assistant, and employee, but equally significant is what he does *not* do. He does not settle in Ripley or follow his father into a farming life. Although his improvisational weave includes a brief return to Ripley as pastor, he soon leaves again, for Georgia, where he lives and works until his death. Mattie, his sister-in-law and then his wife after Hattie dies, closes an imaginary circle in 1925 when she returns Newton's remains to Oberlin. His headstone in Westwood Cemetery, provided by the War Department, arrives three years later (Figure 27).

Oberlin is the right finale: abolitionist hotbed, escape route on the Underground Railroad, origin of the Anti-Saloon League, home to his alma mater. Newton's restless zigzag path concludes not with his arrival at some chosen destination, where he puts down roots, but only with his death, and of course he always believed that his true home is not in this world.

LIFE ON THE ROAD

The war is anything but over. It is not over for the freed slaves who must now discover a new way of life, against the grain of a southern white society that, in an effort to preserve its prerogative and power, turns to terrorism. Records from 1882 show 3,446 African Americans lynched. Nearly two hundred anti-lynching bills die in Congress until, in 2018, an anti-lynching bill is finally approved in the Senate. Far too late and far too little. The bill asserts that between 1882 and 2018 at least 4,742 people are lynched, mostly African Americans. The war is not over for the soldiers who, like Newton, live on bearing its wounds and trauma. It is not over for the families, including countless widows and orphans. The grief in Ohio alone would flood Lake Erie. It is not over for generations of Americans who bear the scars of ongoing racism.

One thousand soldiers in the 101st Ohio Volunteer Infantry—soldiers in name only—march out of Camp Monroeville in September 1862 under the command of Colonel Leander Stem. At the war's end only 329 remain on active duty with the Regiment. Newton Brown and the Huron County boys—the lucky ones who survive dysentery, pneumonia, amputation, and carnage—are now free to scatter where the four winds blow across a battle-scarred land, like them, forever changed.

Acknowledgements

Civil War Duet would not exist without my brother Michael C. Morris. Our often-daily exchanges not only make this book possible. Mike takes the role of editor almost to the point of co-author, and his companionship as we worked together proved an irreplaceable gift.

Mike also deserves full credit for my interest in Newton Brown. In 1996, Mike gave family members bound copies of his original manuscript *J.N.B.* This original research into the life of Reverend Justus Newton Brown later got me started, and it has been a constant resource. Mike too has read every draft, called out innumerable errors, and corrected countless stylistic blunders. Any writer would do well to collaborate with a Bowdoin-educated attorney as editor, proofreader, fact-checker, grammarian, and stylist. Just call Mike. He's really really good.

After all Mike's help, I am left alone on the title page, with pieces of my story to tell as they fall into harmony or dissonance with the life of Newton Brown. Any remaining errors and infelicities I probably slipped in after Mike had corrected what he assumed to be the final draft. Final drafts kept changing and proliferating. Readers lost a talented potential historian, biographer, and storyteller when Mike opted for a career in the law, where facts matter as much as arguments. I hope I have done justice to his indispensable assistance and companionship.

My aim is to tell a story—or multiple intersecting stories—without scholarly endnotes. I have already filled several books with unreadable (and probably unread) citations. I have aimed here for accuracy, but I trust that accuracy need not require a scholarly apparatus citing the innumerable sources, from books to internet sites, to which I'm

ACKNOWLEDGEMENTS

indebted for everything I've learned about the Civil War.

I want to thank Matthew Burr for sharing his knowledge of the 101st Ohio Volunteer Infantry. I owe thanks as well to Louisa C. Hoffman, archival assistant at Oberlin College Archives, and to Maren McKee, collections manager at the Oberlin Heritage Center. Lorie DeWorken provided indispensable help in the design of the text and in working through the numerous revisions. Ellen Morris proved a superb editor, and Dee Morris added incisive suggestions and corrections. Andrew Miller, in a meticulous final reading, provided significant improvements. Jess Morris and Christopher Morris round out my extended-family collaborative Dream Team. Gail Lauzzana and Margot Wolf helped in their own incomparable ways.

I met Margot six months after I started the book and fell headlong in love. Eros and Luck conspired to align. Margot inspires a joy that I had given up hope of finding. It's my misfortune that I short-circuited her contributions by altering successive drafts so quickly that she never got a stable text to improve. It was always in flux. What matters most is that Margot has changed my life in dimensions so crucial as to make thanks irrelevant. I am light years beyond gratitude. I simply could not have kept going and finished this book without her love.

List of Illustrations

FRONTISPIECES

Justus Newton Brown. 1867. Oberlin, Ohio. Photo: H. M. Platt.

David Brown Morris. Photo: Margot Wolf.

Perryville. Our Position At Dark. October 8, 1862 [Detail]. L. W. Day. *Story of the One Hundred and First Ohio Infantry*. Cleveland: W. M. Bayne Printing, 1894.

PART ONE: THE GOOD SOLDIER

Figure 1. George Drake. 1862. Photo: Courtesy of Matthew Burr.

Figure 2. Monroeville (Ohio) Railway Depot. ca. 1862. Photo: Courtesy of Matthew Burr.

Figure 3. *City of Cairo* (Illinois) Steamboat. Built 1864. Cairo Public Library.

Figure 4. Robert E. Lee Monument. 1877. Jean Antonin Mercié, sculptor. Richmond, VA. Photo: David B. Morris.

Figure 5. Jim Crow. Sheet Music. Courtesy of Houghton Library, Harvard College Library.

Figure 6. Frederick Douglass [Detail]. National Archives and Records Administration.

Figure 7. Fort Mitchel, Kentucky. Sketch. 103rd Ohio Volunteer Infantry Civil War Museum, Sheffield Lake, OH. Photo: Courtesy of Matthew Burr.

Figure 8. *Bragg's Invasion of Kentucky* [Detail]. John Formby. *The American Civil War—Maps*. London: John Murray, 1910. Library of Congress Geography and Map Division.

Figure 9. Colonel Leander Stem [Detail]. Hayes Presidential Library and Museums.

LIST OF ILLUSTRATIONS

Figure 10. Reynolds's *Political Map of the United States*. New York: Reynolds and Jones, 1856. Library of Congress Geography and Map Division.

Figure 11. "Out of Bondage" [Illustration to Chapter 43]. E.W. Kemble, illustrator. Mark Twain. *Huckleberry Finn*. New York: Charles Webster and Company, 1885.

INTERLUDE: POSTCOLONIAL AMERICA

Figure 12. Diagram of the Triangular Atlantic Slave Trade. https://goo.gl/images/zrtvSH.

Figure 13. Handbill advertising a slave auction in Charleston, South Carolina. 1769. http://www.greatblacksinwax.org/Exhibits/middle_pass.htm.

PART TWO: LIFE ON THE ROAD

Figure 14. John Brown [Detail]. ca. 1850. Daguerreotype. Detail. Photo: Library of Congress Prints and Photographs Division.

Figure 15. William Lloyd Garrison. 1870. Albumen print. Library of Congress Prints and Photographs Division.

Figure 16. Memorial to Robert Gould Shaw and the Massachusetts Fifty-Fourth Regiment. 1897. Augustus Saint-Gaudens, sculptor. Boston, MA. Photo: National Park Service.

Figure 17. *Little Black Sambo*. 1938. Reprint, Little Color Classics.

Figure 18. *View of Camp Dennison*. Swan & Litchfield, ca. 1865. Library of Congress Prints and Photographs Division.

Figure 19. Bird's Eye View of Camp Chase. Cincinnati: Ehrgott, Forbriger & Co, 1860. Library of Congress and Map Division.

Figure 20. Justus Newton Brown. 1885. Photo: Courtesy of Janet Alkire.

Figure 21. Ruth C. Morris (1944–2016). 2008. Photo: David B. Morris.

Figure 22. Milarepa. Thangka. Photo: David B. Morris.

Figure 23. *Nonviolence ... Our Most Potent Weapon*. 1968. Division of Political History, National Museum of American History, Smithsonian Institution.

LIST OF ILLUSTRATIONS

Figure 24. Southbridge Medical Activities Center. ca. 1969. http://www.hjmc.org/our-heritage.html.

Figure 25. Henrietta Johnson Medical Center. 2018. http://www.hjmc.org.

Figure 26. William James. *Head of a wounded soldier [Garth Wilkinson James] on pillow.* ca. 1863. William James drawings, MS Am 1092.2, (64). Houghton Library, Harvard College Library. https://id.lib.harvard.edu/ead/c/hou02066c00077/catalog.

Figure 27. Gravestone of Justus N. Brown [Detail]. Photo: Courtesy of the Oberlin Heritage Center.

Figure 28. 10-Pound Parrott Rifle. Perryville Battlefield Park, KY. Photo: David B. Morris.

COVER / DUST JACKET IMAGES

Perryville. Our Position At Dark. October 8, 1862 [Detail]. L. W. Day. *Story of the One Hundred and First Ohio Infantry.* Cleveland: W. M. Bayne Printing, 1894.

Justus Newton Brown. 1867. Oberlin, Ohio. Photo: H. M. Platt.

David Brown Morris. Photo: Margot Wolf.

About the Author

DAVID MORRIS is a writer-scholar. He has written two award-winning books on eighteenth-century literature: *The Religious Sublime* (1972) and *Alexander Pope: The Genius of Sense* (1984). *The Culture of Pain* (1991) won a PEN prize and initiated a trilogy that includes *Illness and Culture in the Postmodern Age* (1998) and *Eros and Illness* (2017). He has also lectured and written widely in the field of pain medicine, including a chapter in *Bonica's Management of Pain* (4th & 5th editions) and the co-edited collection *Narrative, Pain, and Suffering* (2005). *Earth Warrior* (1995)—in another departure—tells the story of a ship-ramming anti-driftnet mission with environmental activist Paul Watson. He has held fellowships from the joint NEH/NSF EVIST program, from the American Council of Learned Societies, from the National Endowment for the Humanities, and from the Guggenheim Foundation. He now divides his time between Manhattan and Richmond.

www.ingramcontent.com/pod-product-compliance
Lightning Source LLC
Chambersburg PA
CBHW021942290426
44108CB00012B/935